PRANIC

CRYSTAL HEALING

Oct 18, 2015

Dear Mirtha,

Love meeting you. It is a pleasure. See you again.

Namaste,

Master Marilag

BOOKS WRITTEN BY MASTER CHOA KOK SUI

Miracles Though Pranic Healing

Advanced Pranic Healing

Pranic Psychotherapy

Pranic Crystal Healing

Practical Psychic Self-Defense for Home and Office

Achieving Oneness with the Higher Soul
Meditations for Soul Realization

Universal and Kabbalistic Chakra Meditation
on the Lord's Prayer

The Spiritual Essence of Man

Inner Teachings of Hinduism Revealed

Om Mani Padme Hum
The Blue Pearl in the Golden Lotus

Superbrain Yoga

The Origin of Modern Pranic Healing
and Arhatic Yoga

The Existence of God is Self-Evident

The Chakras and Their Functions

The Golden Lotus Sutras of Master Choa Kok Sui

Beyond the Mind
The Golden Lotus Sutras on Meditation

Inspired Action
The Golden Lotus Sutras on Teaching

Experiencing Being
The Golden Lotus Sutras on Life

Compassionate Objectivity
The Golden Lotus Sutras on Character Building

Creative Transformation
The Golden Lotus Sutras on Spiritual Practice

Achieving the Impossible
The Golden Lotus Sutras on Spiritual Business Management

Possible Miracles
The Golden Lotus Sutras on Pranic Healing

Master Choa Kok Sui

PRANIC
CRYSTAL HEALING

Pranic Crystal Healing

Copyright © 1996 by Master Choa Kok Sui

This printing: October 2012 - 1000 copies

Cover Design and Illustrations by
Benny Gantioqui

Library of Congress Cataloging-in-Publication Data

Sui, Choa Kok
        Pranic Crystal Healing. ----
Makati City, Institute for Inner Studies, Inc. 1996
        182 p.

        1. Magnetic healing. 2. Mental healing.
3. Mind and body. 4. Lasers in medicine
I. title

Fonts used
        Main: Goudy Old Style 12
        Index: Helvetica Narrow 8 / 10

ISBN 971-91106-3-5

Published by
Institute for Inner Studies Publishing Foundation, Inc.
E-mail: iispfi@globalpranichealing.com
Website: www.globalpranichealing.com

Dedicated to

Dabon,

Mike, and

Nene

Acknowledgements

To Divine Providence,
  whose boundless love and blessings
  made this book possible.

To My Respected Teacher Mahaguruji Mei Ling,
  for his blessings and priceless instructions.

To Mike Nator,
  for clairvoyantly monitoring the experiments.

To Others,
  for their valuable suggestions and contributions.

Table of Contents

Master Choa Kok Sui

Introduction

This book embodies the pure essence of the science and art of pranic crystal healing. Ideas or beliefs that are doubtful or superstitious have been removed completely. The concepts, principles, and techniques are based on validated esoteric facts which are explained in a clear and simple manner.

It is assumed that the reader is already knowledgeable and, to a certain extent, proficient in at least elementary pranic healing. Knowledge and proficiency in intermediate pranic healing, advanced pranic healing and pranic psychotherapy will be advantageous.

Nevertheless, the book has been designed in such a way that even a person who is knowledgeable and proficient only in elementary pranic healing or in other forms of energy healing will be able to use it almost instantly.

A crystal is just a tool for healing. Its effectiveness depends on the skill of the pranic healer just as a surgical knife is only a tool whose effectiveness depends on the skill of the surgeon. Although there are many types of crystal that can be used for healing, this book concentrates more on clear quartz crystal.

Pranic Healing Guidelines

1. Pranic Healing is not intended to replace allopathic medicine, but rather to complement it. If symptoms persist or the ailment is severe, please immediately consult a medical doctor and a Certified Pranic Healer.

2. Pranic Healers are not medical doctors, but medical doctors can be Pranic Healers.

3. Pranic Healers should not make medical diagnosis.

4. Pranic Healers should not prescribe medications and/or medical treatments.

5. Pranic Healers should not interfere with the prescribed medications and/or with medical treatments.

6. These Pranic Healing Guidelines must be posted in all Pranic Healing Centers.

CHAPTER ONE

Basic Concepts and Principles

WHAT IS PRANIC CRYSTAL HEALING?

Pranic Crystal Healing is basically using crystal as an instrument in pranic healing.

THREE ESSENTIAL PROPERTIES OF CRYSTALS

What are the three essential properties of a crystal?

1. Subtle Energy Condenser

2. Programmable

3. Chakral Activator

SUBTLE ENERGY CONDENSER

A crystal is a subtle energy condenser. This means that it can absorb, store, project and focus subtle energies. In a certain sense, it is just like a rechargeable battery that can absorb, store and release electrical energy. In the same way, a crystal can absorb, store, project and focus pranic energy.

PROGRAMMABLE

If you look at a natural crystal clairvoyantly, you can see small sparks of light inside. The sparks or points of light are sparks of consciousness. This is a very basic form of consciousness. Synthetic crystals have minimal sparks of consciousness and, as a result, are much inferior when compared to natural crystals.

A crystal does not have any will. Therefore, it follows instructions without resistance. Say "absorb pranic energy" and it absorbs pranic energy. Say "project pranic energy" and it projects pranic energy.

People and animals have consciousness and will power. This is the reason why they may or may not follow your instructions. If you tell them to do something, they can resist. You can command an animal to do something but in some cases the animal will not obey you because it has will power. Even plants have consciousness. Plants tend to grow faster, bigger and healthier when a person talks to them. They have also will power but to a lesser degree.

As stated previously, crystals do not have will power; therefore, they will follow anything you want them to do. When programming a crystal, do not give too many instructions or ask it to do complicated things.

CHAKRAL ACTIVATOR

A crystal is a chakral activator. In other words, it has an activating effect on the chakras. What do we mean by this? When a crystal is placed directly on a chakra, the chakra becomes activated. If you ask a clairvoyant to look at the chakra, it becomes bigger, rotates faster and has more energy. (*See Fig. 1-1*) Not only does the crystal activate the chakra where it has been placed but it also activates other chakras, especially the lower ones.

The following is a suggested experiment:

1. Get a subject, preferably one who is healthy and not pregnant.

2. Sensitize your hands for a few minutes.

3. Scan all the major chakras from the crown to the basic. (See Fig. 1-2)

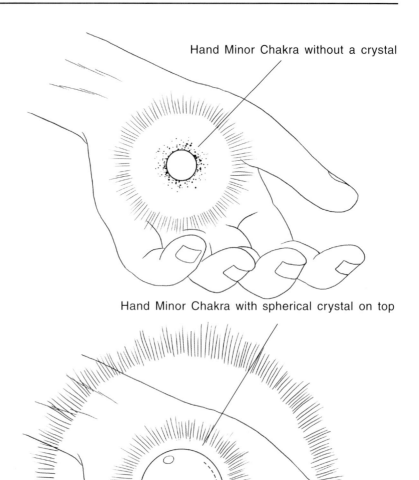

Hand Minor Chakra without a crystal

Hand Minor Chakra with spherical crystal on top

Fig. 1-1 Activating effect of a crystal on the hand chakra

4. Put a big clear quartz crystal on the hand of the subject. If the crystal has a pointed end, position the end towards the subject's body.

5. Scan again all the major chakras from the crown to the basic. Note the changes in the size of the chakras.

6. Scan again the inner aura. Note the changes in the size of the inner aura.

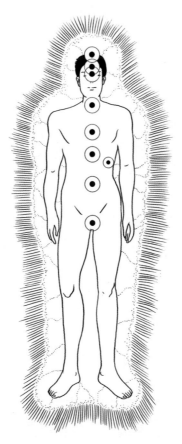

Fig. 1-2   The normal sizes of the chakras and inner aura

You will observe the following:

a)   All the major chakras have become bigger or more activated.

b)   The lower chakras are bigger or more activated than the upper chakras. (See Fig. 1-3)

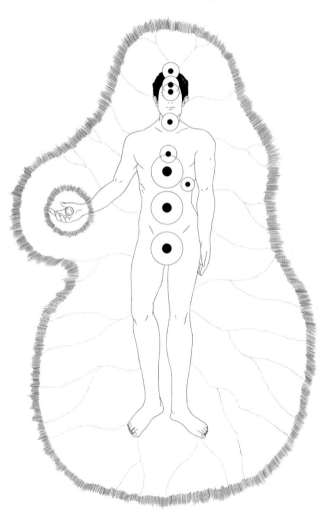

Fig. 1-3   Activating effect of a crystal on the chakras and the inner aura.

c) The inner aura has become bigger.

d) The lower inner aura is bigger than the upper inner aura.

Although crystals have an activating effect on the chakras and tend to make the auras stronger and bigger, they unfortunately tend to activate the lower chakras more than the upper chakras. Notice that the lower chakras are bigger compared to the upper chakras. This implies that patients with heart problems, hypertension or cancer should preferably not have crystals on their body or in the room.

WHEN NOT TO WEAR CRYSTALS

Wearing crystals have certain side effects. You must, therefore know when and where not to wear them. Under what conditions or circumstances should you not wear crystals?

1. Since a crystal has the tendency of activating the lower chakras more than the upper chakras, a person with hypertension should not wear crystals or be near big crystals for a long period of time. Otherwise, the hypertension can become worse or difficult to control. If a person is prone to hypertension, then wearing of crystals is not also advisable.

2. A person with a heart problem should not wear crystals or be near big crystals for a long period of time because this may aggravate the condition.

3. A patient with leukemia should not also wear crystals or be near big crystals for a long period of time because this may also aggravate the condition.

4. When a person has a tumor or cancer, the wearing of crystals is not advisable. In the case of cancer, the basic chakra, the meng mein chakra and the solar plexus chakra are overactivated already. The wearing of crystals will further activate these lower chakras, thereby causing the cancer cells to spread more rapidly.

    A patient who had liver cancer took a medical test after undergoing pranic treatment for many sessions. The results showed the size of the affected part had become substantially smaller. Wanting to get well fast, the patient bought a big amethyst crystal. After one to two weeks, another x-ray test was taken. The doctor was puzzled to discover that the cancer cells had spread even faster.

5. In general, a crystal should not also be worn by people who have mental and psychological imbalances.

6. There is a certain degree of similarity between the chakral condition of a pregnant woman and that of a cancer patient. The basic chakra, the meng mein chakra, and the solar plexus chakra of a pregnant woman are overactivated just like a patient with cancer. The upper chakras of a pregnant woman, however, are normal; in a cancer patient,

the ajna chakra and heart chakra are underactivated. If a pregnant woman wears crystal jewellery, it may further activate the already overactivated lower chakras and may cause hypertension or miscarriage.

Pregnant women should preferably stay away from large quantities of crystals, especially when these crystals have not been cleansed or "processed." They may contaminate and adversely affect the fetus.

7. It is not advisable to wear crystals or be near big crystals when a person is practicing advanced meditation because he is likely to have kundalini syndrome. Kundalini syndrome may manifest in the form of chronic insomnia, chronic physical weakness, pain on different parts of the body, increase in blood pressure and overheating.

Note: *Crystals include diamonds, other precious stones and semi-precious stones.*

The Law of Karma

The Law of Karma states that what a person sows, a person reaps. The science and art of Pranic Crystal Healing, like any other sciences, can be used for good or bad. If utilized for noble purposes, it will generate a lot of good karma for the practitioner. This will manifest as good luck, good health, happiness, prosperity and spirituality. If the teachings and techniques are perverted and misused in order to injure other people, there will be severe karmic repercussions. This will manifest as years of misfortune, poor health, chaos in one's life, and poverty.

Four Basic Techniques in
Processing and Utilizing
a Crystal for Healing

There are four basic techniques used in processing and utilizing a crystal for healing:

1. *Cleansing* is removing dirty energies.

2. *Charging* is putting pranic energy into the crystal.

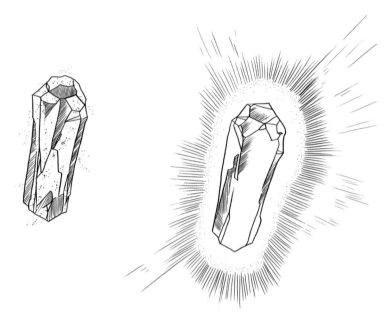

Fig. 2-1   A crystal before and after cleansing

3. *Programming* is giving instruction to the crystal.

4. *Stabilizing* is done so that the absorbed pranic energy will stay longer in the crystal.

CLEANSING A CRYSTAL

It is important to cleanse a crystal before using it. (*See Fig. 2-1*) Why do you have to cleanse it? What are you removing from the crystal?

1. Energy is transferred and absorbed by the crystal everytime a person touches or handles it. The energy could either be

clean or dirty. Using a dirty crystal is just like using a dirty cup for drinking. You have to clean the cup before pouring tea or coffee into it. In the same way, it is not advisable to put clean pranic energy into a dirty crystal. Whatever dirty energy has been put into the crystal has to be removed first.

2. Everytime somebody touches or handles a crystal, a certain quality of the person is transferred to it. Part of the qualities and energies of ordinary people are transferred to the crystals in the process of mining and handling them. This is called psychic impregnation. For instance, if a person holding a crystal has a lot of anger or pessimism, this negative energy will be transferred to or impregnated in the crystal. On the other hand, if the person is positive, that positive quality, in the form of energy, will also be transferred to the crystal. This is the reason why the previous psychic impression or impregnation has to be removed.

3. You also have to remove whatever program has been put into the crystal, if any. The previous owner of the crystal may have already programmed it for certain purposes.

The following is a suggested experiment:

1. Get a crystal that has not yet been cleansed or processed.

2. Sensitize your hands and fingers for a few minutes.

3. Scan the crystal with your right fingers. Please do it very slowly. Feel its energy field. Can you feel the energy of the crystal?

4. Get some of the energy of the crystal using the index and middle fingers. Then move your thumb against the index and middle fingers. Feel the quality of the energy of the crystal that has not been cleansed.

5. Move your left fingers in the same manner.

6. Compare the quality of the energy of the crystal that you feel on your right fingers with the quality of your own energy that you feel on your left fingers.

    Is there any difference between what you feel on the right and the left fingers? How does the dirty energy feel?

    If you are sensitive, you may feel pain, stickiness or a slight discomfort on the right fingers if the crystal is dirty.

How to Cleanse a crystal

There are several ways of cleansing a crystal. To remove the dirty energy, use water and salt, or incense, or both. To remove the psychic impregnation and previous program, use electric violet light through the crown-hand chakras technique. You can also use this technique to remove dirty energy.

Fig. 2-2   Water and salt

WATER AND SALT

What do you do when a place is unlucky? If you are a Catholic, ask a priest to bless it. What does the priest use for blessing? Holy water. What is holy water made of? Water, salt and prayer or "holy energy"

Water and salt can be used to cleanse a crystal. (*See Fig. 2-2*) This can be done in two ways:

1. By soaking the crystal in water and salt for about 30 minutes or more. How much water? About one liter. And how much salt? About a handful. To facilitate the cleansing process, verbally or mentally instruct the crystal to expel the dirty energy while it is being soaked in the salt solution.

2. By rubbing the crystal with your hands in the salt solution for about two to three minutes. While rubbing the crystal with your fingers, there must be an intention to remove the dirty energy. Or you may verbally or mentally instruct the crystal to expel the dirty energy. This method is faster than method number one.

The purpose of washing the crystal with water and salt is to remove the dirty energy. Water has the ability to absorb dirty energy while salt has the ability to break down or disintegrate it.

The following is a suggested experiment:

1. Get a crystal that has not yet been cleansed.

2. Sensitize your hands and fingers.

3. Scan the crystal. Try to feel the quality and the level of energy of the crystal.

4. Wash the crystal with your hands in the salt solution for about three minutes.

5. Dry the crystal.

6. Scan the crystal. Feel the quality and the level of energy of the crystal that has been cleansed.

Cleansing the crystal not only removes the dirty energy but also increases its pranic energy level.

If you have no water and salt for cleansing the crystal, pour or spray ethyl or methyl alcohol on the crystal and rub it with your hand to facilitate the cleansing process. Cleansing with water and salt is more effective than cleansing with alcohol.

If the crystal is of high quality or made of precious stone, do not use water and salt on it because the salt may damage the crystal or precious stone. You can clean it by using cold water only or alcohol, or both.

A crystal that has been used in treating severe ailments will take a longer time to clean since the energy is extremely dirty. To facilitate the cleansing process, instruct the crystal to expel the dirty energy.

INCENSE

Another way of cleansing a crystal is by using incense. When an incense is lighted, it releases certain types of energy. Clairvoyants see the energy as points of light that have certain colors. These colors have corresponding properties.

There are many types of incense. There are incense for love, money, exorcism, and other purposes. One way of cleansing a crystal or a certain place that is etherically dirty is by using a special type of incense. Sandalwood incense, when lighted, produces a green color that has a cleansing effect. The incense used by some churches for exorcism has also a cleansing effect.

Lighting an incense to clean a place or crystal is faster and more powerful if it is accompanied by an intention to clean, or a prayer or

Fig. 2-3   Cleansing a crystal with incense

incantation for cleansing. Just silently will, *"Let this crystal (or place) be cleansed completely."* The cleansing process is faster because the points of light produced by the incense are small beings of light that have consciousness and will, therefore, readily follow your instructions.

How to cleanse a crystal using incense

1. Get a crystal that has not yet been cleansed or processed.

2. Sensitize your hands and your fingers for several minutes.

3. Scan your crystal. Feel the quality of the energy of the crystal.

4. Light a sandalwood incense.

5. Bask the crystal in the smoke of the incense for a few minutes. (*See Fig. 2-3*) Mentally say, *"To the beings of light, please cleanse this crystal of all dirty energy. Thank you for your cooperation."*

6. Scan again the crystal. Feel the quality of the energy of the crystal. Does it feel cleaner and lighter? Is the energy level higher?

Note: *If the reader has a problem in sensitizing and scanning, these steps can be omitted.*

ELECTRIC VIOLET LIGHT

What is the purpose of washing the crystal with water and salt? To remove the dirty energy. Will washing it in salt solution also remove the previous psychic impressions? Partially or maybe not. What about the previous program? Partially or maybe not.

To completely remove the previous psychic impressions and previous program, use electric violet light through the crown-hand chakras technique.

Fig. 2-4   Cleansing a crystal with electric violet light through the crown-hand chakras technique

How to Cleanse a Crystal Using
Electric Violet Light

1. Get a crystal that has not been cleansed or processed.

2. Sensitize your hands and your fingers for several minutes.

3. Scan the crystal. Feel the quality of the energy of the crystal.

4. Connect your tongue to your palate.

5. Concentrate on your crown and your hand.

6. Apply sweeping with electric violet light or brilliant white light on the crystal for about 10 times with the intention of removing all previous psychic impressions and all previous programs. (*See Fig. 2-4*)

7. Scan the crystal. Feel the quality of the energy of the crystal.

How to Cleanse a Crystal Using Prayer

You can also cleanse a crystal using prayer.

1. Get a crystal that has not yet been cleansed or processed.

2. Sensitize your hands and your fingers for several minutes.

3. Scan the crystal. Feel the quality of the energy of the crystal.

4. Concentrate on your crown and your hand.

5. Connect your tongue to your palate.

6. Look at the crystal and pray, *"To the Supreme Being, to the spiritual elders and the holy angels, thank you for cleansing this crystal of dirty energy, previous psychic impressions and previous programs. In full faith. So be it."* Repeat this three times.

7. Simultaneously apply sweeping on the crystal for about 10 times.

8. You may visualize electric violet light or brilliant white light going into the crystal. This step is optional.

9. Scan the crystal. Compare the energy of the crystal against that of your hand. Is it cleaner and lighter?

Note: *If the reader has a problem in sensitizing and scanning, these steps may be omitted.*

In cleansing a crystal, the use of incense is optional. Using water and salt, and electric violet light, however, is necessary. Prayer is extremely helpful.

CHARGING

The technique on how to put pranic energy into the crystal is discussed in Chapter 6.

Programming or Instructing

There are 3 methods of programming or instructing:

1. Verbal - Saying aloud the instructions.

2. Mental - Silently or mentally giving the instruction to the crystal.

3. Use of mind intent - Simply making an intention without the use of words, either verbally or mentally.

Stabilizing

To minimize the escaping of the pranic energy absorbed by the crystal, "paint" the aura of the crystal with light whitish blue or light blue. This is done by just visualizing a light whitish blue film surrounding the crystal or by simply painting the crystal all over with your hand and simultaneously imagining or intending that it is being covered with light whitish blue or light blue. This is called stabilizing. This is necessary to maintain the potency of the crystal.

How to Increase Instantly
Your Healing Power

One of the problems in pranic healing is that a healer sometimes tends to concentrate on the projecting hand and not enough on the receiving hand. As a result, the healer may get depleted. Another problem is that the rate of pranic energy being sucked in by a patient who may be so depleted is much faster than the rate of pranic energy being drawn in by the healer. The healer may become very depleted and will take considerable time to recover. How do you overcome these possible problems?

INCREASING INSTANTLY YOUR HEALING POWER

Based on the following principles, a crystal can be used to increase instantly one's healing power:

1. A *crystal activates the chakras* — the receiving hand chakra and the other chakras of the whole body. (*See Fig. 3-1*)

    By putting a big clear quartz crystal of about 200 grams on the receiving hand chakra, you can increase instantly your healing power by about 100 percent. The receiving hand chakra will be highly activated and will be much bigger than the projecting hand chakra. This will obviously solve the problem of pranic depletion of the healer due to concentrating too much on the projecting hand and not enough on the receiving hand.

    Another effect of putting a big crystal on the receiving hand is that all the other chakras are activated and the lower chakras become about twice bigger, thereby increasing the capacity of the healer to absorb and project a lot of pranic energy. The rate of pranic energy absorbed by the healer will be higher than the rate of pranic energy sucked in by the patient. This is of course the solution to the possible problem of the healer being depleted when healing a very weak patient.

Fig. 3-1 Increasing your healing power instantly by placing a sphere crystal on the receiving hand when healing.

2. *A crystal increases the intensity or density of pranic energy that is absorbed and projected by the chakras and the energy body.*

The bigger a crystal, the higher is its degree of chakral activation and the higher also is the intensity or density of the pranic energy that is absorbed and projected. For example, if the average size of a chakra is about three inches, putting a quartz crystal on the receiving hand can double the average chakral size. However, when the weight of a crystal is between 100-200 grams, the degree of chakral activation plateaus or levels off. At 400 grams, the increase in the degree of activation becomes minimal but (1) the density of the energy body is increased, and (2) the density or intensity of pranic energy that is absorbed and projected is also higher. In other words, the degree of activation between a 200-gram and 400-gram crystal is almost the same. The effect of a 400-gram crystal, however, is not only in the density or intensity of pranic energy that is absorbed and projected by the chakras but also in the energy body.

In general, using crystals of about 100-200 grams is sufficient to increase substantially one's healing power. Using a 400-gram crystal is advantageous but it is a little bit heavy since the healer may have to hold the crystal on his or her hand for several hours. If the healer does not mind the discomfort due to the weight of the crystal, then it is perfectly all right to use a 400-gram or 500-gram crystal.

A suggested experiment:

1. Scan the thickness and diameter of your hand chakra. Can you feel the energy of your palm?

2. Put a clean clear quartz crystal on your receiving hand.

3. Scan again the thickness and diameter of your hand chakra. Notice that it has become thicker and wider in radius.

How do you increase instantly your healing power?

4. Get a big clear quartz crystal weighing about 200 grams.

5. Cleanse the crystal thoroughly. This is very important to avoid contamination and increase the activating effect of the crystal.

6. Put the crystal on the receiving hand with the sharp end pointing towards you. Why should the sharp end of the crystal be pointed towards you? This is because the direction of the flow of pranic energy is affected by the direction of the sharp end of the crystal. Since you want the pranic energy to flow towards you, not away from you, the sharp end of the crystal, therefore, has to be pointed towards you.

7. Curl the tip of the tongue and let it touch your palate. A crystal tends to overactivate the lower chakras. By connecting the tongue to the palate, this effect is reduced substantially, thus making the lower chakras only slightly bigger than the upper ones.

8. With a clean clear quartz crystal on the receiving hand, use the projecting hand for general sweeping, localized sweeping, and energizing. This will at least double your healing power and reduce the amount of time required to treat a patient.

After healing, be sure to wash thoroughly your projecting hand and arm to remove the diseased energy or to decontaminate yourself. Washing the receiving hand and arm to remove the excess pranic energy is also advisable.

All the rules and guidelines in elementary, intermediate, and advanced pranic healing should be followed in pranic crystal healing. This is very important.

SHAPES OF CRYSTALS USED AS CHAKRAL ACTIVATOR

You may use a crystal as a chakral activator with the following shapes: sphere, single terminated and double terminated.

For single terminated crystals, the pointed end should be towards you, the healer. (*See Fig. 3-2*) When using a double terminated crystal, it should be put across the palm. (*See Fig. 3-3*)

Fig. 3-2 *Increasing your healing power instantly by placing a crystal on the receiving hand when healing. When holding a single terminator quartz crystal, the sharp end of the crystal should be pointing towards you.*

Fig. 3-3　*Increasing your healing power instantly by placing a*
crystal on the receiving hand when healing. When using
a double terminator quartz crystal, put it across the
palm.

FIVE THINGS TO AVOID IN PRANIC HEALING

(The following text is taken from **Miracles Through Pranic Healing***, originally titled "The Ancient Science and Art of Pranic Healing" by* **Master Choa Kok Sui** *to serve as a reminder to pranic healers, and as precautionary guidelines for healers belonging to other disciplines as well as for readers with no healing background at all.)*

1. Do not apply too intense and too much prana on infants, very young children, or very weak and elderly patients. With infants and very young children, their chakras (energy centers) are still small and not quite strong. Very weak and elderly patients have chakras that also are weak. Applying too much prana or energizing too intensely will result in a choking effect on their chakras. This is similar to the choking reaction of a very thirsty person who drinks too much water in too short a time. Infants and children should be energized gently and gradually and only for a short period of time. Their chakras, being quite small, can easily be overenergized and congested. The ability of very weak and old patients to assimilate prana is very slow. Therefore, these types of patients should be energized gently, gradually, and for a longer period of time since their bodies are quite depleted. They should be allowed to rest and assimilate prana for about 15-20 minutes before energizing them again.

If the solar plexus chakra is suddenly overenergized, resulting in the choking effect on the chakra, the patient may suddenly become pale and may have difficulty breathing. Should this happen, apply localized sweeping immediately on the solar plexus area.

The patient will be relieved immediately. This type of case is rare and is presented only to show what to do in case something like this happens.

2. Do not energize the eyes directly. The eyes, being delicate, will be easily congested with prana if energized directly and may be damaged in the long run. The eyes can be energized through the back of the head (backhead chakra), the area between the eyebrows (ajna chakra), and the temples (temple chakra). In case the eyes are sufficiently energized, the excess prana would just flow to other parts of the body.

3. Do not energize directly and intensely the heart for a long time. It is quite sensitive and delicate. Too much prana and too intense energizing may cause severe pranic congestion of the heart. The heart should be energized through the back of the spine near the heart area. In energizing the heart through the back, prana flows not only to the heart but to other parts of the body. This reduces the possibility of pranic congestion on the heart. If the heart is energized through the front, the flow of prana is localized around

the heart area, thereby increasing the possibility of pranic congestion.

4. Do not energize the meng mein chakra of infants, small children, and older people. This may activate the meng mein chakra and cause the infant, small child or elderly patient to have hypertension which may affect the brain in the process. With pregnant women, this chakra should not also be treated since it may cause adverse effects on the unborn child. This chakra should be energized only by advanced or experienced pranic healers.

5. Do not energize the spleen chakra of infants or children because they may faint as a result of pranic congestion. Should this happen, apply general sweeping several times to remove the excess pranic energy. The spleen chakras of patients with hypertension or a history of hypertension should not also be energized because the patient's condition might become worse. However, this chakra is used to treat patients who are very weak or those with severe infections. It is important that the spleen chakra should be energized only by advanced or experienced pranic healers.

Pranic healing is quite safe as long as you follow properly the given guidelines and instructions.

FACTORS DETERMINING

THE POTENCY OF A CRYSTAL

Different crystals have different degrees of potency. If it is very clear, it is more powerful. A clear quartz crystal is more powerful than a milky or smoky quartz crystal. A rose quartz is non-transparent and less powerful than clear crystal but since it is pink, its pranic energy is easily assimilated by the patient. This makes the healing process faster.

Besides the clarity of a crystal, the size, and whether the crystal has been charged/consecrated does not determine its degree of potency. A bigger crystal is more powerful than a small one. A small crystal, however, can be extremely powerful if it has been properly consecrated.

RING WITH CRYSTAL(S) AS CHAKRAL ACTIVATOR

Is it possible to further increase the activating effect of clear quartz crystal? In other words, is it possible to increase the power of the crystal? The answer is yes. This is done by thoroughly cleansing the crystal and consecrating it. How to consecrate the crystal will be discussed in Chapter 6.

If you find bringing a big clear quartz crystal inconvenient or holding it on your receiving hand as tiring, would it be possible to substitute it with a ring that has a crystal? The answer is yes.

1. This is done by cleansing the crystal thoroughly. A clean crystal has a greater activating effect than a dirty crystal.

2. The crystal used for a ring must be of very good quality. A 2.5-gram or less clear quartz crystal of gem quality, or even small semi-precious stones of very good quality have an activating effect almost similar to a 100-gram ordinary clear quartz crystal.

It is important that you wear the crystal ring on the proper finger. What finger should you use? The ring finger. What is the reason for this? Each finger corresponds to certain chakra(s). If you put it on the other fingers, certain chakras may get partially overstimulated and the corresponding delicate organs may eventually be partially affected. The energy may pass to the heart chakra or the crown chakra or some other chakras that control and energize certain delicate organs of the body; this may eventually create to a certain degree unnecessary health problem(s). When you wear a crystal on the ring finger, the energy simply passes from the hand to the throat chakra with minimal or no adverse effect, except for people with hyperthyroidism.

What crystal stones can you use? You can use clear quartz, amethyst, rose quartz, green tourmaline, and others.

With clear quartz, you can project white prana or color pranas. With rose quartz, the pranic energy is tinged with pink. This is good for treating psychological disorders or physical ailments that are

***Fig. 3-4   Increasing your healing power instantly by using two
          rings with crystals***

psychological in origin. The pranic energy is also easily assimilated
by the patient. Amethyst, on the other hand, emits violet or electric
violet light.

Green tourmaline or emerald is good because it gives off green
pranic energy that has a cleansing effect. Green tourmaline is better

than emerald because (1) it is cheaper; and (2) the projected green pranic energy is relatively darker than that of emerald. With emerald, the projected green pranic energy is too light. Diamond, although it produces electric violet light, may be too forceful. Unless a healer is skilful and can soften the projected energy, then the healing process may be slowed down. With garnet, the projected energy is dark red. In general, it is not suitable for healing unless the healer deliberately dilutes the projected dark red pranic energy with a lot of white prana.

If you want to be more powerful, you can wear two rings of similar crystals. (*See Fig. 3-4*) But your receiving hand should have a ring with a bigger crystal so that the pranic energy absorbed is more than the pranic energy given out. In this way, you are less likely to be depleted. It is very important that the "crystal ring" should be consecrated properly to increase its power. See Chapter 6 for detailed instructions.

It is advisable for pranic healers or people in the health field to wear a green tourmaline daily on the receiving hand. This not only increases one's healing power but also minimizes the possibility of contamination due to diseased energy.

The precious and semi-precious stones or crystals must preferably not be sharp or pointed at the bottom. This will cause pranic energy to leak out from the energy body. The bottom must be rounded or flat.

CHAPTER FOUR

How to Cleanse and Energize
With a Laser Quartz Crystal

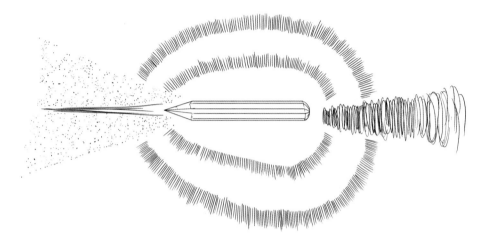

Fig. 4-1 Laser crystal

LASER CRYSTAL

A "laser quartz crystal" is not really a laser. It is just a label given to a long thin quartz crystal with a pointed tip. (*See Fig. 4-1*) Sometimes the end of the crystal may have two pointed tips. The pranic energy that comes out of the pointed tip is focused or concentrated while the surrounding portion is dispersed.

A laser crystal can be used for cleansing and energizing. When the tip of the laser crystal is used for cleansing, it is like using high-pressured water to clean the floor. The concentrated energy of the laser crystal makes cleansing more effective. A laser crystal should preferably be about five and one-half inches in length to allow for easy handling and to minimize contamination of the healer.

HOW TO HOLD A LASER CRYSTAL

There are two ways of holding a laser quartz crystal:

(*See Fig. 4-2*)

1. Hold the laser crystal between the thumb, the forefinger and the middle finger with the receiving end inside the palm. When it is held this way, the crystal projects pranic energy from the hand chakra and the finger chakras.

2. Hold the laser crystal with the same set of fingers (as in number one) but with the receiving end outside the palm. The projected pranic energy comes mainly from the finger chakras.

You may choose either method, whichever you would prefer.

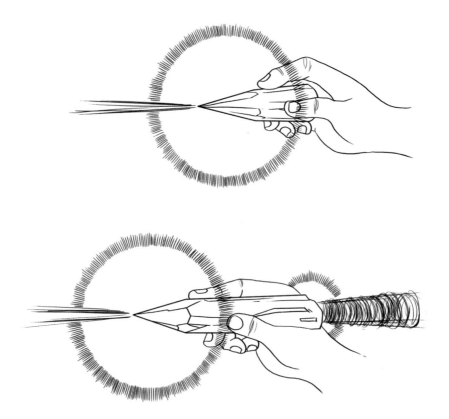

Fig. 4-2 Two ways of holding a laser crystal

CHAKRAL ACTIVATOR ON THE RECEIVING HAND
AND LASER CRYSTAL ON THE PROJECTING HAND

Instead of using the projecting hand for general sweeping, localized sweeping, and energizing, you can use a laser crystal. This will substantially minimize contamination from diseased energy.

When treating a patient, put a chakral activator crystal on your receiving hand and a laser crystal on the other hand. (*See Fig. 4-3*)

*Fig. 4-3   Using a crystal ball on the receiving hand and a laser
crystal on the projecting hand.*

The chakral activator crystal should be bigger and heavier than the laser crystal. This method will increase your healing power. The cleansing is faster and the time required in treating a patient per session is shorter.

The following crystals may be used as a chakral activator: crystal ball, single terminated or a double terminated crystal.

When projecting pranic energy, the healer may project white prana by visualizing white light or color prana by visualizing color light. The healer may visualize white light or may not visualize anything at all when projecting white prana.

The laser crystal has to be cleansed thoroughly after treating a patient. This is to avoid contaminating the next patient. It can also be cleansed, if necessary, while treating the patient.

HOW TO DO GENERAL SWEEPING
WITH A LASER CRYSTAL

Using a laser quartz crystal for general sweeping is similar to the way general sweeping is done in basic pranic healing.

1. Put a big clear quartz crystal on the receiving hand and a laser crystal on the projecting hand.

2. Apply sweeping with the laser crystal on line one from top to bottom. Move the crystal straight down and do this slowly. When sweeping, form an intention to re-move the diseased energy. Flick the diseased energy to the disposal unit or the basin of water and salt. (See Fig. 4-4)

3. Apply sweeping with your laser crystal on line two at the right side and line two at the left side.

4. Proceed in this manner on lines three, four, and five.

5. Apply sweeping on the back. To cleanse thoroughly, apply general sweeping two to three times.

Instead of moving the laser crystal straight down, you may move the laser crystal in a slight zigzag motion downward. (See Fig. 4-5) This has a greater cleansing effect.

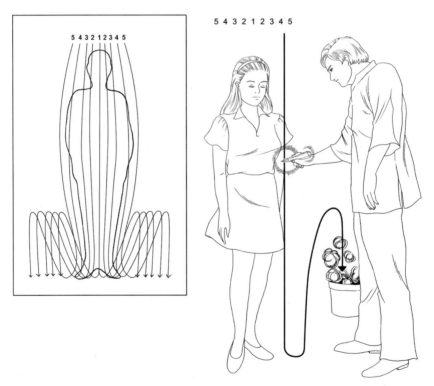

Fig. 4-4   *General sweeping with a laser crystal in a straight downward motion*

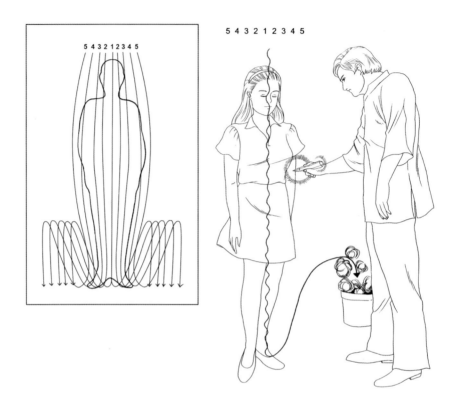

***Fig. 4-5   General sweeping with a laser crystal in a slight zigzag
downward motion***

HOW TO DO LOCALIZED SWEEPING

WITH A LASER CRYSTAL

You can do localized sweeping using any of the following five
methods:

1. Apply sweeping with the laser crystal in a *straight downward
   motion* on the affected part or chakra. Do this five times

then flick the diseased energy into the disposal unit. Repeat the process about seven times or more. (*See Fig. 4-6*)

2. Apply sweeping with the laser crystal in a *slight zigzag motion* downward on the affected part or chakra. Do this five times then flick the diseased energy into the disposal unit. Repeat the process about seven times or more. (*See Fig. 4-7*)

3. Apply a *broad zigzag motion* with your laser crystal on the affected part or chakra. Do this five times then flick the diseased energy into the disposal unit. When sweeping, form gently an intention to remove the diseased energy. Repeat the process about seven times or more. (*See Fig. 4-8*)

4. Apply a *clockwise motion* with your laser crystal to project pranic energy on the affected part or chakra for a few seconds. Then move the laser crystal *counterclockwise* to cleanse the affected part or chakra for a few seconds. When sweeping, gently form an intention to remove the diseased energy. Flick the diseased energy into the disposal unit. If the affected chakra is congested, more counterclockwise motion should be applied than the clockwise motion. A rough guideline would be about two times more of the counterclockwise than the clockwise motion. If the chakra is depleted, the clockwise motion should roughly be two times more than the counterclockwise motion. (*See Fig. 4-9*)

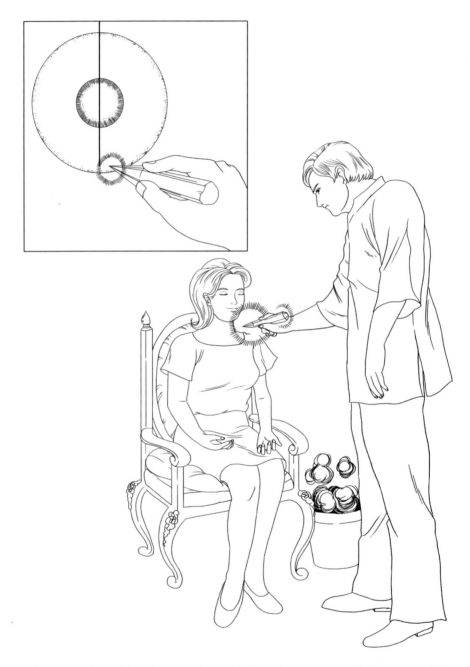

Fig. 4-6   Localized sweeping with a laser crystal in a straight downward motion

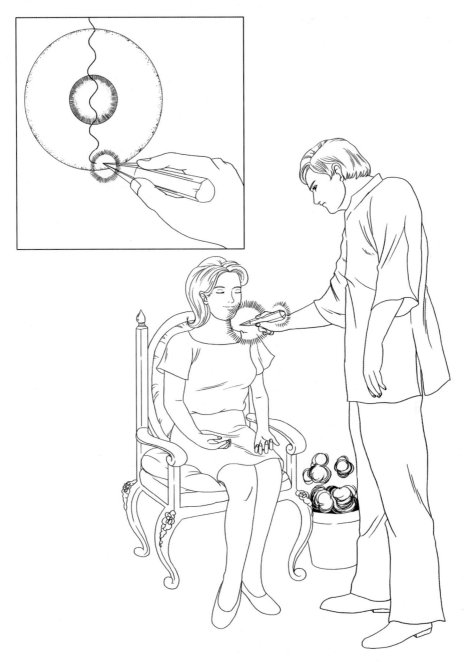

Fig. 4-7   *Localized sweeping with a laser crystal in a slight zigzag motion*

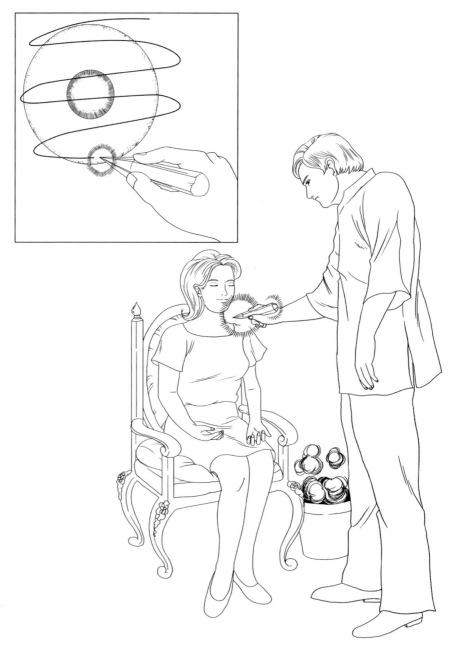

Fig. 4-8   Localized sweeping with a laser crystal in a broad zigzag motion

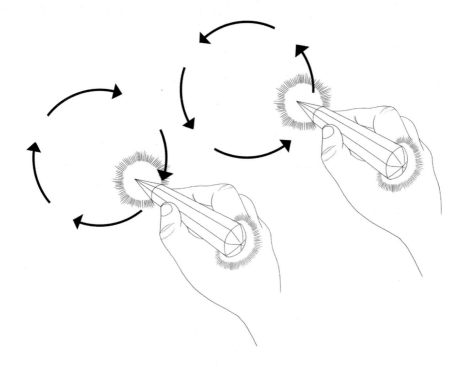

*Fig. 4-9   **Moving the laser crystal in a clockwise motion to
facilitate the projection of pranic energy; moving the
laser crystal in a counterclockwise motion to facilitate
the removal of diseased energy***

5. If the affected part or chakra is very dirty, disintegrate the
   diseased energy by puncturing it with the laser crystal. This is
   called "puncturing the diseased energy technique." It is done
   through mind intent and by pointing the sharp tip of the
   laser crystal from a distance at the affected part or chakra,
   then moving it back and forth in a "puncturing" motion.
   Repeat this process many times. This will loosen or disintegrate the diseased energy to facilitate the cleansing process.

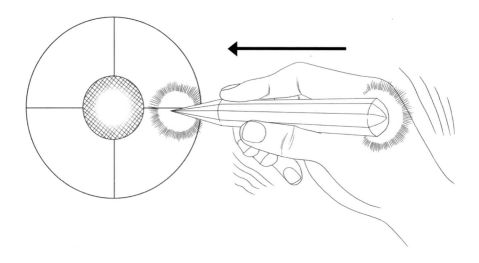

Fig. 4-10 Puncturing the diseased energy technique

Apply localized sweeping with the laser crystal to remove the diseased energy. Flick the diseased energy into the disposal unit. Clean thoroughly by alternately disintegrating the diseased energy and sweeping the affected part or chakra. Repeat the whole process about 20 times or more. (*See Fig. 4-10*)

Note: *When using the puncturing technique, avoid using too much will because the organ or chakra being treated might be literally damaged. Use only a little will. This is very important. Please remember this.*

How to Cleanse a Dirty Chakra Thoroughly

To cleanse a very dirty chakra thoroughly, "divide" it into six parts. What is meant by dividing a chakra into six parts? A chakra on the surface is more or less circular. Imagine dividing it into five sections – the right upper section, the left upper section, the left lower section, the right lower section, and the center. The sixth section is the inner section which makes up the stem and the root of the chakra. (*See Fig. 4-11*)

On the right upper section, disintegrate the diseased energy and apply localized sweeping five times. Flick the diseased energy into the disposal unit. Repeat the same procedure on the left upper section, the left lower section, the right lower section and then the center. Repeat the whole process about seven times or more. Apply the whole process on the inner section — the stem and the root of the chakra. Repeat this about seven times or more. This is called the "six-section chakral cleansing technique".

In severe ailments, some chakras are extremely dirty. You can achieve rapid healing by cleansing them thoroughly. This is very important.

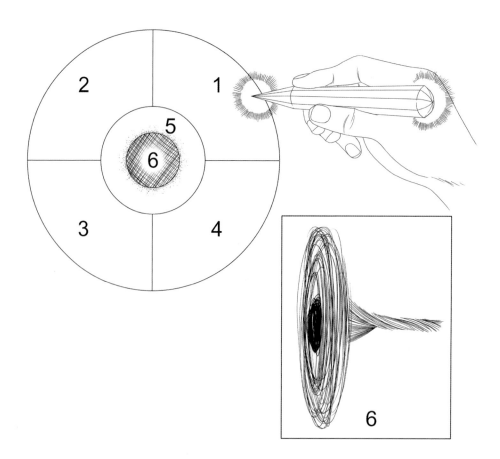

Fig. 4-11 "Six-section chakral cleansing technique"

      (1) Right upper section

      (2) Left upper section

      (3) Left lower section

      (4) Right lower section

      (5) Center

      (6-Inset) Stem and root of the chakra

How to Energize with the Use of a Laser Crystal

1. Put a big clear quartz crystal on the receiving hand and a laser crystal on the projecting hand.

2. Point the laser crystal at the affected part or chakra that you want to energize.

3. Flick the diseased energy regularly from the laser crystal to the disposal unit.

4. How do you know when the affected part or chakra has been sufficiently energized? When energizing with the hand, it is easy to feel the repulsion or the cessation of flow of pranic energy. When energizing with a laser crystal, there is lesser sensitivity. Therefore, you have to increase your awareness to heighten your sensitivity or you can regularly scan with your hand to determine whether it has been sufficiently energized.

How to Stabilize the Projected Pranic Energy

(This instruction is repeated for the sake of readers with no background in pranic healing.)

The projected pranic energy, unless stabilized, tends to escape within 30 minutes to several hours. This is the reason why sometimes symptoms recur within a short period after pranic treatment.

How do you stabilize the projected pranic energy? After projecting the pranic energy, stabilize it by mentally painting the treated part with light blue or light sky blue for a few seconds. You may move your hand or the laser crystal in a painting motion on the treated part.

HOW TO CUT THE LINK

(This instruction is repeated for the sake of readers with no background in pranic healing.)

Visualize a link between you and the patient. The link is seen clairvoyantly as a thin cord of light connecting your solar plexus chakra and the patient's solar plexus chakra. To cut the link, just imagine your hand or the laser crystal like a knife and mentally cut the cord of light.

INVOKING FOR DIVINE BLESSINGS

To make the healing safer, faster and more effective, it is advisable to invoke for divine blessings before healing the patient. (*See Fig. 4-12*)

> *To the Supreme Being,*
> > *Thank You for the divine guidance,*
> > *for the divine love and mercy,*
> > *for healing this patient,*
> > *for the divine help and protection.*
> > *With thanks and in full faith* (4x).

Fig. 4-12 Divine healing energy passes through the healer and the crystal when invoking for divine blessings.

To the healing angels, healing ministers, spiritual teachers, spiritual elders, beings of light, and the great ones,

> *Thank You for the divine guidance,*
> *for the divine love and mercy,*
> *for healing this patient,*
> *for the divine help and protection.*
> *With thanks and in full faith* (4x).

You may use your own words or your own prayer. At the end of the treatment, it is advisable for the healer to say a short prayer of thanksgiving.

To the Supreme Being,

> *Thank You very much for the blessings,*
> *and for healing this patient.*
> *With thanks and in full faith* (4x).

> *Thank You also for assigning a healing angel*
> *and a healing minister to the patient*
> *until healing is complete.*
> *With thanks and in full faith* (4x).

To the healing angels, healing ministers, spiritual teachers, spiritual elders, beings of light, and the great ones,

> *Thank you very much for the blessings,*
> *and for healing this patient.*
> *With thanks and in full faith* (4x).

Note: Repeat the words *"With thanks and in full faith"* four times, *not the whole prayer.*

The rate of healing can be further accelerated if the patient says a short prayer requesting for healing before the start of the treatment and another short prayer at the end of the treatment. The patient may use his or her own words.

Before the start of the treatment, the patient may use this prayer:

To the Supreme Being,

> *Thank You for Your divine blessings,*
> *for the divine love and mercy,*
> *for divine healing,*
> *for the divine help and protection.*
> *With thanks and in full faith* (4x).

To the healing angels, healing ministers, spiritual teachers, spiritual elders, beings of light, and the great ones,

> *Thank you for your divine blessings,*
> *for the divine love and mercy,*
> *for divine healing,*
> *for the divine help and protection.*
> *With thanks and in full faith* (4x).

At the end of the treatment:

To the Supreme Being,

> *Thank You again for the divine blessings,*
> *and for the divine healing.*
> *With thanks and in full faith* (4x).

To the healing angels, healing ministers, spiritual teachers, spiritual elders, beings of light, and the great ones,

> *Thank you again for the divine blessings,*
> *and for the divine healing.*
> *With thanks and in full faith* (4x).

DISTRIBUTIVE SWEEPING

You may apply distributive sweeping at the end of the treatment. This will further accelerate the rate of healing by:

1. improving pranic energy circulation; and

2. facilitating the spread of pranic energy to the different parts of the body.

How do you do this?

1. After treatment, apply distributive sweeping up and down on the front of the body. Apply distributive sweeping from the crown down to the sex chakra, then from the sex chakra upward to the crown. Do this slowly and repeat about 5 times. (*See Fig. 4-13, 1*)

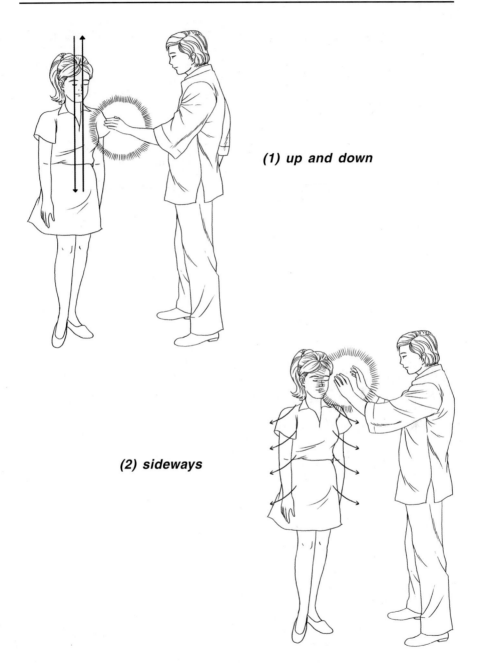

(1) up and down

(2) sideways

Fig. 4-13 Distributive sweeping on the front of the body

2. Apply distributive sweeping sideways. Raise both hands together near the face of your patient. Move your hands sideways to the right and to the left. Go to the throat area and move your hands sideways to the right and to the left. Go to the chest area and repeat the same process until you reach the sex chakra. (See Fig. 4-13, 2)

3. Ask the patient to turn around and apply distributive sweeping up and down on the back of the body. Then apply distributive sweeping sideways. Follow the instructions in steps 1 and 2. (See Fig. 4-14, 3 & 4)

4. Apply distributive sweeping on the arms and the legs. (See Fig. 4-14, 5)

CRYSTAL DISTANT HEALING

Can you use a crystal for pranic distant healing? Yes.

1. Put a chakral activator on the receiving hand and a laser crystal on the projecting hand.

2. Imagine the patient is in front of you about 12 inches in height. The visualization does not have to be clear. What is important is the intention to send the healing energy to this particular patient. (See Fig. 4-15)

3. Apply general sweeping and localized sweeping. When sweeping, repeat the name of the patient regularly. This is to make the cleansing process more effective.

(3) up and down

(4) sideways

(5) on the arms and legs

Fig. 4-14 Distributive sweeping on the back of the body

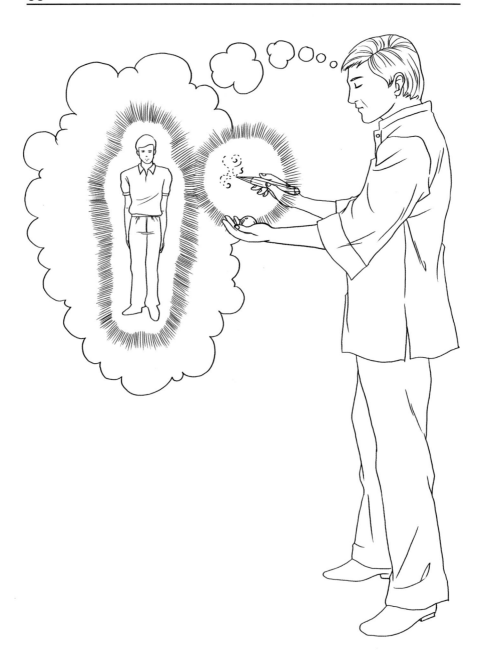

Fig. 4-15 Using a crystal for distant healing

4. Repeat also the name of the patient regularly when energizing. This is to ensure that most of the healing energy goes to the patient, not just out to the universe.

5. Repeat the treatment several times a week for as long as necessary.

You may invoke for divine blessings before healing. Healing should not be done when the patient is driving, handling heavy equipment or doing a critical task that may affect his safety or that of others.

USING THE CRYSTAL AS AN EXTRACTOR

A crystal is a subtle energy condenser. Therefore, it can absorb both pranic energy and diseased energy. Since a crystal is also programmable, you can instruct it to extract, absorb, disintegrate and expel dirty energy, diseased energy, negative elementals and negative thought entities from an affected part or chakra. You may use a small piece of clear quartz, or a green tourmaline. A green tourmaline is more effective as an "extractor" since green has a disintegrating effect.

The keywords are *extract, absorb, disintegrate* and *expel*. In giving instruction to a crystal, you have to be exact and thorough. For example, if you just say "extract," it will just extract but it will not absorb, disintegrate and expel. You also have to specify to the crystal to extract dirty energy and diseased energy, not the clean pranic energy; specify also which chakra or part of the body is to be cleansed. In other words, you should tell the crystal exactly what to do. The crystal will not perform a specific task unless you instruct it to do so.

The place used must be well ventilated so that diseased energy can be carried away from the healing area. It is also advisable to clean the healing room with sandalwood incense.

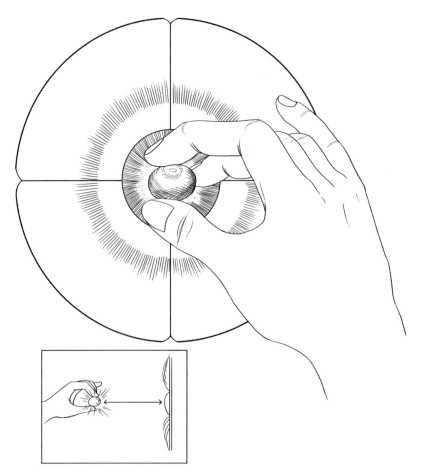

Fig. 4-16 Holding a pebble-sized crystal extractor near an affected chakra

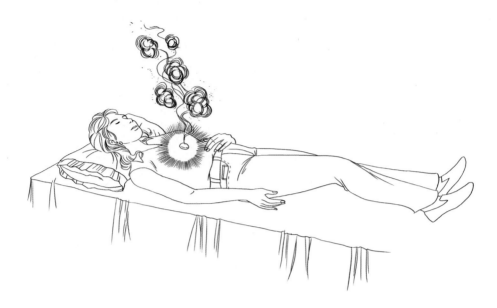

Fig. 4-17 Using a crystal to extract stress energy from the solar plexus chakra

TWO WAYS OF USING THE EXTRACTOR

You can use the extractor in two ways:

1. Hold the crystal near the affected part or chakra. If the patient is lying down, put the extractor on the affected part or chakra, then instruct it to extract, absorb, disintegrate and expel the diseased energy. (*See Fig. 4-16 & 17*) If you are doing pranic psychotherapy, you also have to instruct the crystal to extract, absorb, disintegrate and expel the negative thought entities and negative elementals. Wait for

a certain period of time, then flick the diseased energy into the disposal unit. Instruct the extractor to stop by mentally or verbally saying "stop." Clean the extractor thoroughly.

2. Hold the extractor near the affected part or chakra. Move it clockwise and simultaneously project pranic energy through it for a few seconds. Then move the extractor counterclockwise and simultaneously instruct it to extract, absorb, disintegrate and expel the diseased energy. Flick the diseased energy into the disposal unit. Repeat this process several times until the affected part or chakra is relatively clean. Then instruct the extractor to stop.

ALLOW ENOUGH TIME FOR THE EXTRACTOR TO WORK

A crystal can extract diseased energy only at a certain rate. Therefore, it should be given enough time to complete its work.

For example, if you have too much stress or tension, you can just lie down and put a green tourmaline on your solar plexus. Instruct the crystal to extract, absorb, disintegrate and expel all stress energy and diseased energy from the solar plexus chakra and the whole body. Rest for 15 to 20 minutes, and then instruct the crystal to stop. You will probably feel a lot better after this. You may also use rose quartz for stress instead of green tourmaline since rose quartz has pink prana that has a soothing and calming effect.

If the patient is lying down, you can put several extractors on different parts of the body and give them the proper instructions. This will make cleansing the different affected chakras and affected parts, including the whole body, a lot easier for the healer. If you have many patients, let several of them lie down, then put extractors on them to help and facilitate the cleansing process. More of this topic will be discussed under Chapter 7.

APPLICATIONS

As stated earlier, it is assumed that you are already knowledgeable and proficient in pranic healing. There will be some readers, however, with no background in pranic healing or energy healing. Therefore, for purposes of clarification and convenience, a few examples will be given on how to heal several common ailments and disorders. In applying the following treatment procedures, project white prana unless the color is specified.

Simple Ailments and Disorders

How do you treat simple ailments and disorders?

1. Put the chakral activator on your receiving hand and the laser crystal on the projecting hand.

2. Connect your tongue to your palate.

3. Apply localized sweeping with the laser crystal in a slight zigzag motion on the affected part. Do this five times, then flick the dirty energy into the disposal unit.

4. Repeat step 3 seven times.

5. Energize sufficiently the affected part. If you are not sensitive enough to determine whether the affected part has been fully energized or not, just energize it for about three to five minutes.

6. If the patient is still not relieved substantially, apply localized sweeping and energizing again once or twice.

7. If symptoms persist, the patient is either not receptive or the ailment might be more severe than it seems. Therefore, instruct the patient to see a medical doctor and a proficient advanced pranic healer.

8. Stabilize by mentally painting the treated part with light blue pranic energy for a few seconds, then cut the etheric link between you and the patient.

Wounds

1. Put the chakral activator on the receiving hand and the laser crystal on the projecting hand. (*See Fig. 4-18*)

2. Connect your tongue to your palate.

3. Apply localized sweeping with the laser crystal in a slight zigzag motion on the affected part. Do this five times, then flick the dirty energy into the disposal unit.

4. Repeat step 3 seven times.

5. Energize the affected part for about five to 10 minutes.

6. Stabilize by mentally painting the treated part with light

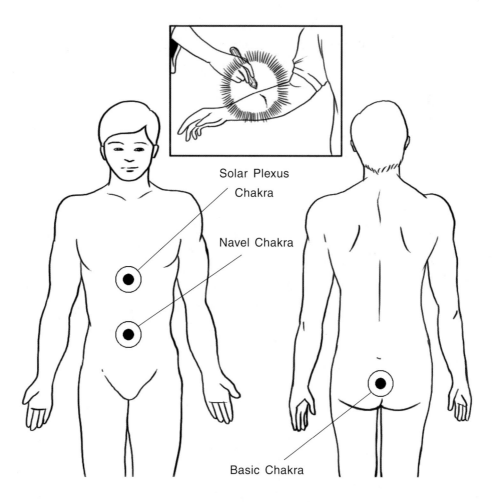

Solar Plexus
Chakra

Navel Chakra

Basic Chakra

Fig. 4-18 Pranic treatment for the healing of wounds

blue pranic energy for a few seconds, then cut the etheric link between you and the patient.

7. You may repeat the treatment three times a day for rapid miraculous healing.

8. If the patient has a problem with the healing of a wound, then the basic chakra, navel chakra and solar plexus chakra should also be treated.

Fresh Burns

1. Put the chakral activator on the receiving hand and the laser crystal on the projecting hand.

2. Connect your tongue to your palate.

3. Apply localized sweeping with the laser crystal in a slight zigzag motion on the affected part. Do this five times, then flick the dirty energy into the disposal unit.

4. Repeat step 3 seven times or more until the pain is reduced substantially.

5. Energize the affected part for about three to five minutes.

6. Repeat the cleansing and energizing process until it is completely healed.

7. Stabilize by mentally painting the treated part with light blue pranic energy for a few seconds, then cut the etheric link between you and the patient.

8. Instruct the patient not to wash the treated part for two days and not to put any cream on it, especially vitamin E cream. The application of vitamin E cream on freshly-burned skin will cause it to blister. Vitamin E cream can be applied on an old burn but not on a new one that has been given pranic treatment.

For old burns, the procedure is almost the same. The treatment can be repeated three times a day to accelerate the healing process. The basic chakra can be treated to further hasten the rate of healing.

Toothache

1. Put the chakral activator on the receiving hand and the laser crystal on the projecting hand.

2. Connect your tongue to your palate.

3. Instruct the patient to point one finger on the affected part.

4. Apply localized sweeping with the laser crystal in a straight downward motion on the affected part, instead of a slight zigzag motion. Do this five times, then flick the dirty energy into the disposal unit.

5. Repeat step 4 seven times. After cleansing, the patient may experience partial or complete relief.

6. Energize the affected part for about three to five minutes.

7. Stabilize by mentally painting the treated part with light blue pranic energy for a few seconds. Cut the etheric link between you and the patient.

8. Even if the patient is completely relieved, instruct the patient to see a dentist.

Menstrual Discomfort

1. Put the chakral activator on the receiving hand and the laser crystal on the projecting hand.

2. Connect your tongue to your palate.

3. Apply localized sweeping with the laser crystal in a slight zigzag motion on the sex chakra or on the pubic area. Do this five times, then flick the dirty energy into the disposal unit.

4. Repeat step 3 seven times. In most cases, the patient will experience substantial relief.

5. You may energize the sex chakra for a few minutes.

6. For more complete and permanent healing, the basic chakra, perineum minor chakra, navel chakra, solar plexus chakra, throat chakra and ajna chakra have to be treated. (*See Fig. 4-19*)

7. Stabilize by mentally painting the treated part with light blue pranic energy for a few seconds. Cut the etheric link

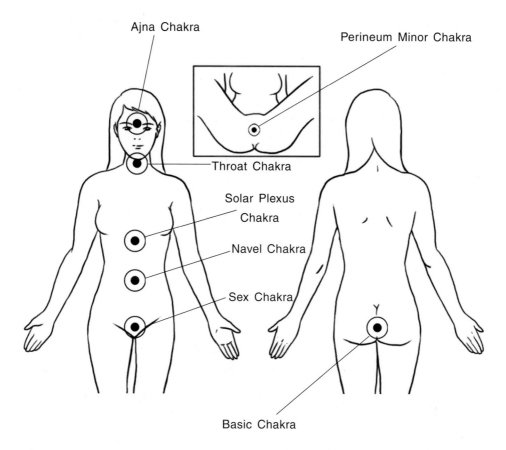

Ajna Chakra

Perineum Minor Chakra

Throat Chakra

Solar Plexus
Chakra

Navel Chakra

Sex Chakra

Basic Chakra

Fig. 4-19   Pranic treatment for menstrual discomfort

between you and the patient.

8. The treatment can be done three days before the menstrual
    period to minimize or prevent the discomfort from
    occurring.

Enlarged Prostate

The sex chakra, perineum chakra, and the prostate are affected. They have to be cleansed and energized thoroughly. The prostate is located just on top of the perineum. (*See Fig. 4-20*)

1. Put the chakral activator on the receiving hand and the laser crystal on the projecting hand.

2. Connect your tongue to your palate.

3. Apply localized sweeping with the laser crystal in a slight zigzag motion on the sex chakra which is located above the

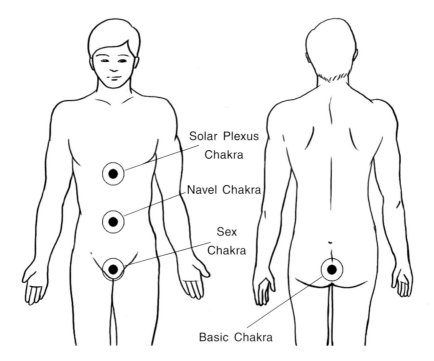

Solar Plexus
Chakra

Navel Chakra

Sex
Chakra

Basic Chakra

Fig. 4-20 Pranic treatment for enlarged prostate

perineum. Do this five times, then flick the dirty energy into the disposal unit.

4. Repeat step 3 seven times.

5. Energize the sex chakra for a few minutes.

6. Cleanse and energize thoroughly the perineum minor chakra and the prostate. This is important for more thorough and complete healing.

7. The basic chakra, the navel chakra and the solar plexus chakra are partially affected. Cleanse and energize them.

8. Stabilize by mentally painting the treated part with light blue pranic energy for a few seconds. Cut the etheric link between you and the patient.

9. Repeat the treatment two to three times a week. Most patients will notice rapid improvement.

Abdominal Pain, Vomiting, and Loose Bowel Movement

1. Put the chakral activator on the receiving hand and the laser crystal on the projecting hand.

2. Connect your tongue to your palate.

3. Apply general sweeping two to three times with the laser crystal.

4. Apply localized sweeping with the laser crystal in a slight zigzag motion on the solar plexus chakra and the upper

abdominal area. Do this five times, then flick the dirty energy into the disposal unit. (*See Fig. 4-21*)

5. Repeat step 4 seven times.

6. Apply localized sweeping with the laser crystal in a slight zigzag motion on the navel chakra and the lower abdominal

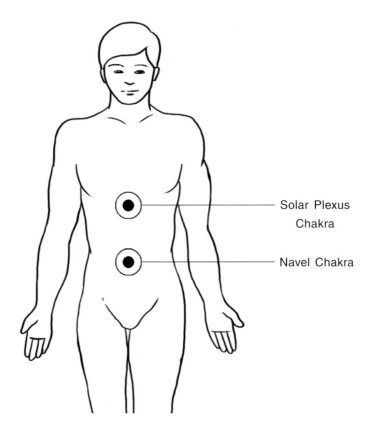

Solar Plexus
Chakra

Navel Chakra

Fig. 4-21 Pranic treatment for abdominal pain, vomitting, and loose bowel movement

area. Do this five times, then flick the dirty energy into the disposal unit.

7. Repeat step 6 seven times. The patient may experience instant relief and cure just by cleansing thoroughly the solar plexus chakra, navel chakra, and the upper and lower abdominal areas, even without energizing.

8. Energize the solar plexus chakra and the navel chakra for a few minutes.

9. Stabilize by mentally painting the treated part with light blue pranic energy for a few seconds. Cut the etheric link between you and the patient.

10. In severe cases, repeat the treatment two to three times a day for the next several days.

In severe cases or if symptoms persist, instruct the patient to consult a medical doctor immediately and to have pranic treatment by a more experienced, proficient pranic healer.

When treating gastrointestinal ailments, it is important to clean the patient thoroughly before energizing. Otherwise, the patient may experience radical reaction or the condition may become worse temporarily.

Headache

TREATMENT FOR HEADACHE IN GENERAL:

1. Put the chakral activator on the receiving hand and the laser crystal on the projecting hand.

2. Connect your tongue to your palate.

3. Ask the patient which part of the head is painful.

4. Apply localized sweeping thoroughly with the laser crystal on the affected part(s). If cleansing is done thoroughly, the pain will be reduced substantially. (*See Fig. 4-22*)

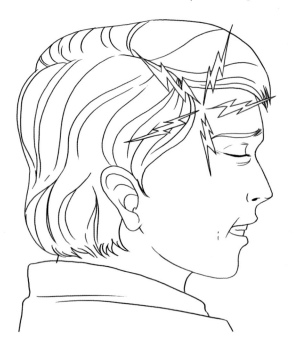

Fig. 4-22 Headache

5. Energize the affected part(s) for a few minutes.

6. Stabilize then cut.

HEADACHE DUE TO STRESS:

If the headache is due to stress or some emotional problems, the solar plexus chakra must be cleansed thoroughly. (*See Fig. 4-23*)

1. Put the chakral activator on the receiving hand and the laser crystal on the projecting hand.

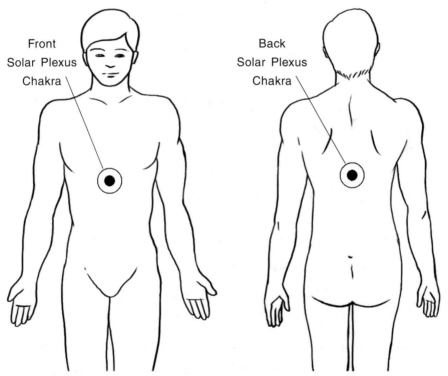

Fig. 4-23 Pranic treatment for headache due to stress

2. Connect your tongue to your palate.

3. Apply localized sweeping with the laser crystal on the front solar plexus chakra. Do this five times. Flick the dirty energy into the disposal unit.

4. Repeat step 3 seven times.

5. Apply localized sweeping with the laser crystal on the back solar plexus chakra. Do this five times, then flick the dirty energy into the disposal unit. Repeat the whole process seven times. Once the solar plexus chakra has been cleansed thoroughly, the patient will experience partial relief.

6. Energize the front and back solar plexus chakras for a few minutes.

7. Apply localized sweeping thoroughly on the affected parts of the head area and energize.

8. Stabilize then cut.

HEADACHE DUE TO EYE STRAIN:

1. Scan the eyes, the temples and the ajna chakra. Apply localized sweeping thoroughly using your hand(s). It is preferable not to use the chakral activator and the laser crystal when cleansing the eyes directly since they might be energized or overenergized. This may cause the condition to become worse after a certain period of time. (*See Fig. 4-24*)

2. Connect your tongue to your palate.

3. Put the chakral activator on the receiving hand and the laser crystal on the projecting hand.

4. Apply localized sweeping on the back head area with the laser crystal.

5. Energize the eyes through the back head and the ajna chakra.

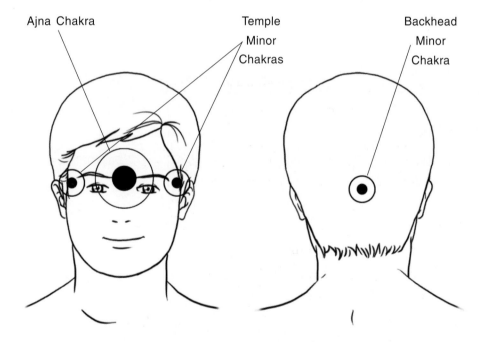

Fig. 4-24 *Pranic treatment for headache due to eye strain.*

6. Apply localized sweeping thoroughly on the affected parts of the head and energize.

7. Stabilize then cut.

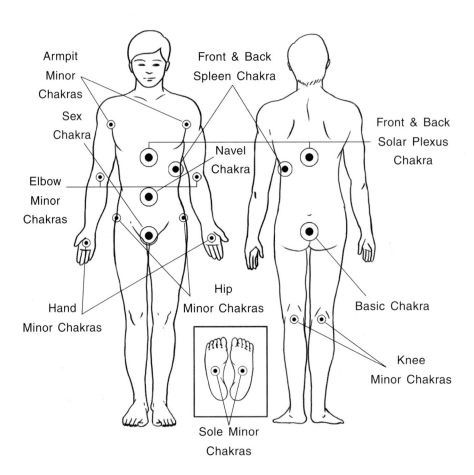

Armpit
Minor
Chakras

Front & Back
Spleen Chakra

Sex
Chakra

Front & Back
Solar Plexus
Chakra

Navel
Chakra

Elbow
Minor
Chakras

Hand
Minor Chakras

Hip
Minor Chakras

Basic Chakra

Knee
Minor Chakras

Sole Minor
Chakras

Fig. 4-25 Pranic treatment for arthritis

Arthritis

1. Put the chakral activator on the receiving hand and the laser crystal on the projecting hand.

2. Connect your tongue to your palate.

3. Apply general sweeping three times.

4. Apply localized sweeping and energizing thoroughly on the basic chakra, perineum minor chakra, sex chakra, navel chakra, front and back solar plexus chakras and the liver. (*See Fig. 4-25*)

5. If the patient has rheumatoid arthritis, the front and back spleen chakra must be cleansed and energized. This has to be done gently and carefully because some patients may faint if the spleen chakra is overenergized. On rare cases, the blood pressure may go up.

6. If the affected part is in the arm, then its minor chakras must be treated; if the leg is affected, its minor chakras must be treated.

7. Apply localized sweeping thoroughly on the affected part(s). Energize it for about five to 10 minutes.

8. Stabilize by mentally painting the treated part with light blue pranic energy for a few seconds. Cut the etheric link between you and the patient.

9. You may repeat the treatment three times a week for about three months.

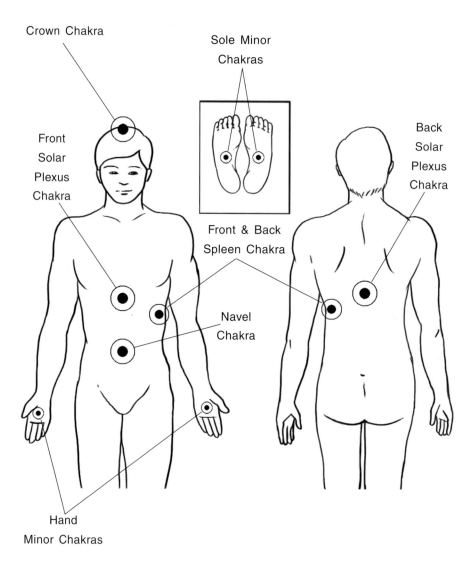

Fig. 4-26 Pranic treatment for fever

Fever

Based on clairvoyant observations, the whole body of a person who has fever is depleted and surrounded by a thin greyish red aura. The front and back solar plexus chakras are congested and filled with dirty red energy. By removing the greyish red energy from the whole body, and by decongesting and removing the dirty red energy from the front and back solar plexus chakras, the fever will subside very quickly. The basic chakra should not be energized directly since this will make the temperature go up. (*See Fig. 4-26*)

About 70-80% cases of fevers are caused by either respiratory infections or by gastrointestinal infections. If the patient has a stuffy nose, cough or sore throat, and/or difficulty in breathing, then the patient may have respiratory infection. If the patient has abdominal pain, vomiting, loose bowel movement and/or blood in the stool, the patient may have gastrointestinal infection.

In women, fever could be due to urinary tract infections. The symptoms are pain and difficulty in urination, pain and discomfort on the pubic area, and/or pain on the lower back.

1. Put the chakral activator on the receiving hand and the laser crystal on the projecting hand.

2. Connect your tongue to your palate.

3. Apply general sweeping five times with the laser crystal.

4. Apply localized sweeping with the laser crystal in a slight zigzag motion on the front solar plexus chakra. Do this five times, then flick the dirty energy to the disposal unit. Repeat this step 10 times.

5. Apply localized sweeping in a slight zigzag motion on the back solar plexus chakra. Do this five times, then flick the diseased energy into the disposal unit. Repeat this step 10 times.

6. Energize the front and back solar plexus chakras for a few minutes.

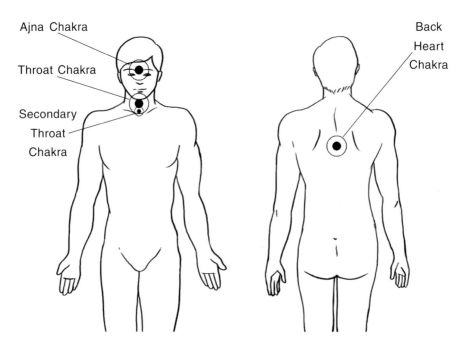

Fig. 4-27 Pranic treatment for fever due to respiratory infection

7. Apply localized sweeping thoroughly on the upper and lower abdominal areas.

8. In case of severe infection, apply localized sweeping and energizing on the front and back spleen chakra with caution.

9. Apply localized sweeping and energizing on the navel chakra, crown chakra, hand minor chakras, and sole minor chakras.

10. If the fever is due to respiratory infection, apply localized sweeping and energizing on the ajna chakra or the nose, the

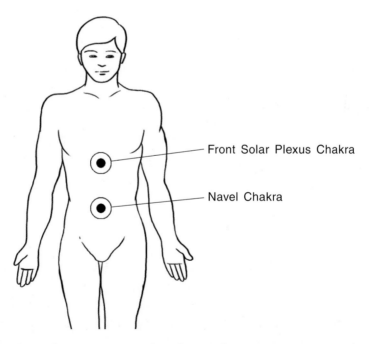

Front Solar Plexus Chakra

Navel Chakra

Fig. 4-28 Pranic treatment for fever due to gastrointestinal infection

throat chakra and the secondary throat chakra, the lungs, and the back heart chakra. (*See Fig. 4-27*)

11. If the fever is due to gastrointestinal infection, apply localized sweeping thoroughly on the liver, stomach, small intestine, and large intestine. Apply localized sweeping and energizing on the navel chakra. (*See Fig. 4-28*)

12. If the fever is due to urinary tract infection, apply localized sweeping and energizing thoroughly on the sex chakra (pubic area). If there is lower back pain, apply localized sweeping

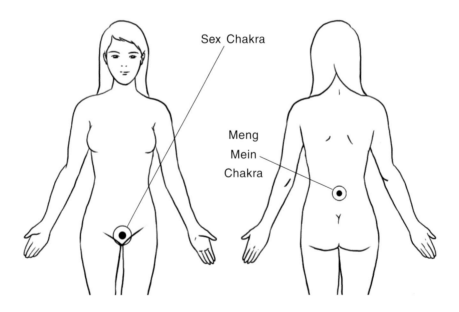

*Fig. 4-29 **Pranic treatment for fever due to urinary tract infection***

thoroughly on the kidneys and the ureters. Put the chakral activator and laser crystal down. Apply localized sweeping with your hand on the meng mein chakra for about 30 times. This is to minimize the possibility of the blood pressure from going up. (*See Fig. 4-29*)

13. If the fever is due to tonsillitis, apply localize sweeping and energizing thoroughly on the jaw minor chakras, throat chakra, and secondary throat chakra. (*See Fig. 4-30*)

14. Stabilize then cut.

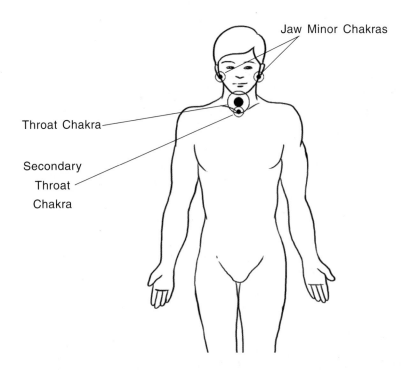

Fig. 4-30 Pranic treatment for fever due to tonsillitis

15. Repeat the treatment twice a day for the next few days.

16. If the ailment is severe or symptoms persist, instruct the patient to consult immediately a medical doctor and a proficient pranic healer.

Hypertension

1. Put the chakral activator on the receiving hand and the laser crystal on the projecting hand.

2. Connect your tongue to your palate.

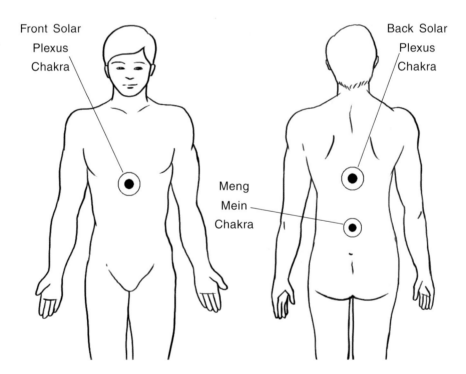

Fig. 4-31 Pranic treatment for hypertension

3. Apply general sweeping five times.

4. Apply localized sweeping thoroughly on the front and back solar plexus chakras with light green prana. To clean them, use the "puncturing the diseased energy technique" and the "six-section chakral cleansing technique." Cleanse also the liver thoroughly.

5. Energize the front and back solar plexus chakras with light whitish green prana, then with light blue prana. Mentally instruct them to become smaller if they are still overactivated after thorough cleansing. (*See Fig. 4-31*)

6. Put the chakral activator down. Use the laser crystal only. Apply localized sweeping thoroughly on the meng mein chakra with light green prana. Use the "puncturing the diseased energy technique" and the "six-section chakral cleansing technique".

7. Energize the meng mein chakra with light whitish prana, then with more light blue prana. Mentally instruct the meng mein chakra to become smaller. The size of the meng mein chakra should be about 1/3 - 1/2 of the back heart chakra.

8. If done properly, there will be substantial improvement.

Note: *The procedure given above is only for practitioners of advanced pranic healing.*

Heart Problems

1. Put the chakral activator on the receiving hand and the laser crystal on the projecting hand.

2. Connect your tongue to your palate.

3. Apply general sweeping three times.

4. Apply localized sweeping thoroughly on the front and back solar plexus chakras with light green prana. Use the "six-section chakral cleansing technique." Cleanse also the liver

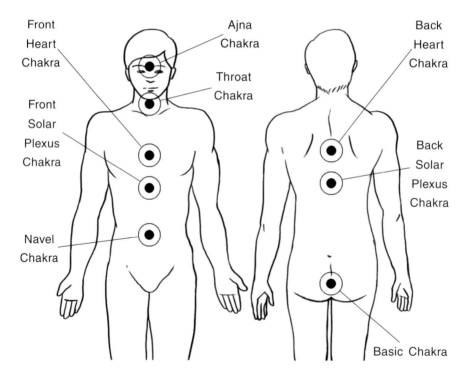

Fig. 4-32 Pranic treatment for heart problems

thoroughly. (*See Fig. 4-32*)

5. Energize the front and back solar plexus chakras with light whitish green prana, then with light blue prana. If they are still overactivated after thorough cleansing, mentally instruct them to become smaller.

6. Put the chakral activator down. Scan the front heart chakra and the physical heart. Use your hand or the laser crystal only for localized sweeping with light green prana on the front heart chakra. For thorough cleansing on the heart chakra, even though it is not very dirty, use the "six-section chakral cleansing technique."

7. Put the chakral activator on the receiving hand and the laser crystal on the projecting hand.

8. Apply localized sweeping and energizing on the back heart chakra.

9. If the patient is a heavy smoker, apply localized sweeping thoroughly, using green prana on the back of the lungs and the side of the lungs. Apply localized sweeping thoroughly on the back heart chakra with light green prana, using the "puncturing the diseased energy technique" and the "six-section chakral cleansing technique." After this, energize the back heart chakra with white prana.

10. Apply localized sweeping and energizing on the basic chakra,

navel chakra, throat chakra, and the ajna chakra.

11. Stabilize, then cut.

12. Repeat the treatment two to three times a week for two to three months.

Multiple Sclerosis

According to medical doctors, multiple sclerosis is due to chronic inflammation, destruction of the outer covering of the nerves (myelin) of the central nervous system and scarring. This results in weakness of the arms and legs, inability to coordinate voluntary movements, numbness, visual blurring, and double vision, among other symptoms. Memory loss is common in advanced multiple sclerosis.

The chakral conditions of a person with multiple sclerosis are the following:

1. The front and back solar plexus chakras are extremely overactivated, dirty and usually congested.

2. The spleen is depleted.

3. The spine is etherically dirty.

4. The basic chakra and sex chakra are very overactivated but depleted. The perineum minor chakra is dirty. Both the meng mein and navel chakras are small and depleted. By cleansing and energizing the navel chakra, it is easier and faster to normalize the meng mein chakra, sex chakra, and

basic chakra, including the perineum minor chakra.

5. The heart chakra is slightly underactivated; the throat chakra
    is overactivated but depleted. The jaw minor chakras are
    dirty and may be congested. The ajna, the forehead chakra,
    the crown chakra and the back head minor chakra are
    dirty, underactivated and congested. The forehead chakra
    is sometimes overactivated but depleted. The areas of the
    brain above the ears are usually congested.

By applying advanced pranic healing thoroughly, there may be
noticeable or dramatic improvement in one to five sessions if the
ailment is not too severe.

Procedure:

1. Scan the patient thoroughly. Then observe his or her physical
    condition before the treatment.

2. Apply localized sweeping thoroughly on the front, side and
    back of the lungs. Do "cleansing and strengthening the
    blood technique" by energizing through the back of the
    lungs with light whitish green, light whitish orange and light
    whitish red. The proportion should be about four breathing
    cycles for light whitish green, three breathing cycles for light
    whitish orange, then about seven breathing cycles for light
    whitish red. Stabilize by painting the lungs with light whitish
    blue on the outside. Should the patient experience radical
    reaction in the form of chest pain, apply localized sweeping

thoroughly on the front and back heart chakras until the pain disappears. In future treatments, it is important to make the projected color prana lighter in shade if the patient has experienced chest pain.

3. Do "cleansing and strengthening the internal organs technique." Project light whitish blue first, then light whitish green, light whitish orange, and light whitish red. Energize the front solar plexus with light whitish blue for one breathing cycle, light whitish green for three breathing cycles, light whitish orange for three breathing cycles and light whitish red for six breathing cycles. Apply the same procedure on the back solar plexus chakra. Let the patient rest for about three minutes to enable the projected pranic energies to cleanse and energize the other chakras.

4. Rescan the upper and lower chakras. You will notice that by doing the "cleansing and strengthening the blood technique" and "cleansing and strengthening the internal organs technique," the condition of the chakras has improved. The basic chakra and the sex chakra that were overactivated and depleted will become less overactivated and more energized. The navel chakra and the meng mein chakra will be more activated and more energized. The upper chakras that are usually small and congested will become bigger and less congested. Using "cleansing and strengthening the blood technique," and "cleansing the internal organs technique"

is very important for rapid healing of multiple sclerosis.

5. Apply general sweeping about three to four times.

6. Apply localized sweeping thoroughly on the navel chakra with light whitish green prana. Energize thoroughly with light whitish green for about three breathing cycles, then with light whitish red for about eight breathing cycles. This step is very important since the proper functioning of the other lower chakras depends on the proper functioning of the navel chakra. If the navel chakra is cleansed and energized thoroughly, the other lower chakras will improve substantially.

7. Apply localized sweeping thoroughly on the basic chakra, sex chakra, and perineum minor chakra with light whitish green and light whitish orange. Energize each one of them thoroughly with light whitish red for about eight breathing cycles.

8. Apply localized sweeping thoroughly on the meng mein chakra with green prana, then energize with white prana for about four to five breathing cycles. Rescan the meng mein chakra. If it is overactivated, remove the excess energy until the chakra becomes normal. With older people, just energize the meng mein chakra with white prana for about two breathing cycles. The healer has to be careful with patients who are over 55 years old since over energizing the meng

mein chakra may cause some problems.

9. Apply localized sweeping on the spleen chakra with light whitish green and light whitish violet. Then energize with light whitish violet prana for about three to five breathing cycles. Rescan the spleen chakra and the meng mein chakra. Energizing the spleen chakra can sometimes cause the meng mein chakra to become overactivated. If this happens, inhibit the meng mein chakra immediately by applying localized sweeping on the meng mein chakra and the spleen chakra.

10. Apply localized sweeping thoroughly on the front and back heart chakras. Then energize the back heart chakra with light whitish green for three breathing cycles and light whitish violet for six breathing cycles. The heart chakra affects the proper functioning of the upper chakras. By cleansing and energizing it, the healing process of the upper chakras is facilitated.

11. Apply localized sweeping thoroughly on the right and left areas of the brain, slightly above the ears, with light green prana alternating with light whitish violet. The jaw minor chakras also have to be cleansed thoroughly with light whitish green, alternating with light whitish violet.

12. Apply localized sweeping on the throat chakra, ajna chakra, forehead chakra, crown chakra, and back head minor chakra

with light whitish green and light whitish violet. Then energize each one of them with light whitish green for about three breathing cycles, light whitish violet for about four breathing cycles and light electric violet prana for one breathing cycle. The breathing cycle for electric violet can be increased gradually to two after several weeks of treatment. This will facilitate the healing process in the brain area. Rescan the chakras.

13. Apply distributive sweeping up and down on the back of the patient, from the crown to the base of the spine, for about 10 times. Then apply distributive sweeping up and down on the front of the body from the crown to the sex chakra for about 10 times. Distributive sweeping is very important because it improves energy circulation and brings the sex energy and basic energy to the upper chakras. The upper chakras are fed by the energies of the sex chakra and the basic chakra. Their proper functioning depends on the availability of the sex and basic energies.

If you rescan the upper chakras, after doing distributive sweeping, you will note that the upper chakras have become much bigger. This method can also be used for healing mentally retarded children or adults

Rescan the sex chakra and the basic chakra. You will note that these chakras might be partially depleted. If they are, energize them with light whitish red.

14. Apply localized sweeping on the front and back solar plexus chakras. Energize the front and back solar plexus chakras with white prana for seven breathing cycles.

15. Apply localized sweeping on the arms and legs alternately with light whitish green and light whitish orange. Then energize the arms and legs through the minor chakras: armpit, elbow, hand, hip, knee and sole chakras with light whitish green for two breathing cycles, light whitish orange for two breathing cycles and light whitish red for five breathing cycles.

Numbness on the toes and fingers or on other parts of the body can be removed substantially by cleansing with light whitish green and light whitish orange, and energizing with light whitish green, light whitish orange, and light whitish red.

Repeat the treatment three times a week and gradually reduce it to two times a week. Continue the treatment for three to six months. For severe multiple sclerosis, the treatment might take about six months or longer. In general, the patient will show remarkable, if not miraculous, improvement.

The number of breathing cycles given is just simply a general guideline. The healer must make the necessary adjustments on the instructions given based on how powerful the healer is and the requirements and condition of the patient. A powerful healer can project sufficient color prana in a matter of a few seconds while an ordinary healer will require several breathing cycles.

The procedure for the treatment of multiple sclerosis should be done preferably by an experienced advanced pranic healer.

How to Use Crystals for
Color Pranic Healing

This chapter is written for advanced pranic healers as guidelines on how to use crystals to project color pranas. It also serves as an introduction to color pranic healing. For a more in-depth study, please read *Advanced Pranic Healing* by *Master Choa Kok Sui.*

PROJECTING COLOR PRANAS WITH
A LASER CRYSTAL

Color pranas can be projected using a clear quartz crystal. You can use a natural laser quartz crystal or a clear quartz crystal that has been cut and shaped into a laser crystal. The pranic energy coming out of a clear laser crystal is "white" prana; therefore, it is easy to use for projecting color pranas.

How do you project color pranas using laser crystal?

1. Put a chakral activator on the receiving hand and a laser crystal on the projecting hand.

2. Connect your tongue to your palate.

3. To project a color prana, concentrate on the major chakra that contains the required color prana and your fingertips simultaneously. You may also concentrate simultaneously on the center of the palm of the projecting hand. This is optional. Concentrating on the tips of the fingers is sufficient.

4. There are three techniques for projecting color pranas:

    a) Basic-hand chakras technique

    b) Throat-hand chakras technique

    c) Crown-hand chakras technique

BASIC-HAND CHAKRAS TECHNIQUE

The basic-hand chakras technique uses the basic chakra as the source chakra and the hand chakra as the projecting chakra. (*See Fig. 5-1*)

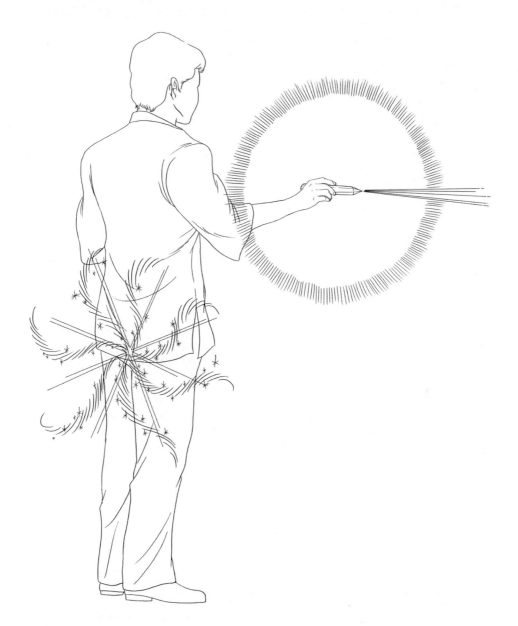

Fig. 5-1   Basic-hand chakras technique using a crystal

To do this technique, concentrate on the basic chakra and the projecting hand. Concentrate on or be aware of the base of your spine and the tips of the projecting fingers simultaneously. Imagine or visualize the required color prana(s).

Using the basic-hand chakras technique, you can project the following color pranas. Each color prana has corresponding properties:

1. Red prana — warm, expansive, strengthening, and activating

2. Orange prana — expelling, and cleansing

3. Gross yellow prana — cementing or joining; stimulates growth.

4. Orange-red prana — rapid healing of fresh wound.

5. Orange-yellow prana — rapid healing of broken bones and torn tendons.

Procedure:

1. Put the chakral activator on your receiving hand, and the laser crystal on your projecting hand.

2. Connect your tongue to your palate.

3. Concentrate on or be aware of the base of your spine and the tips of the projecting fingers.

4. To produce light whitish red prana, project white prana first by visualizing white light through the laser crystal. Mentally add light red prana to the white light and mix them together. Visualize and project light whitish red prana.

5. Follow the same technique for projecting light whitish orange and light whitish yellow.

6. To produce light whitish orange-red prana, project white light, then mentally add light red to the periphery of the white light and add light orange to the periphery of the periphery of the light red. There should be slightly more light red than light orange.

7. To project light whitish orange-yellow prana, use the same technique for producing light whitish orange-red prana.

THROAT-HAND CHAKRAS TECHNIQUE

The throat-hand chakras technique uses the throat chakra as the source chakra and the hand chakra as the projecting chakra and the projecting hand chakra. Be aware of your throat and concentrate simultaneously on the tips of the projecting fingers. Visualize the required color prana(s). (*See Fig. 5-2*)

The throat-hand chakras technique is used to project the following color pranas with their corresponding properties:

1. Green prana — breaking down, cleansing

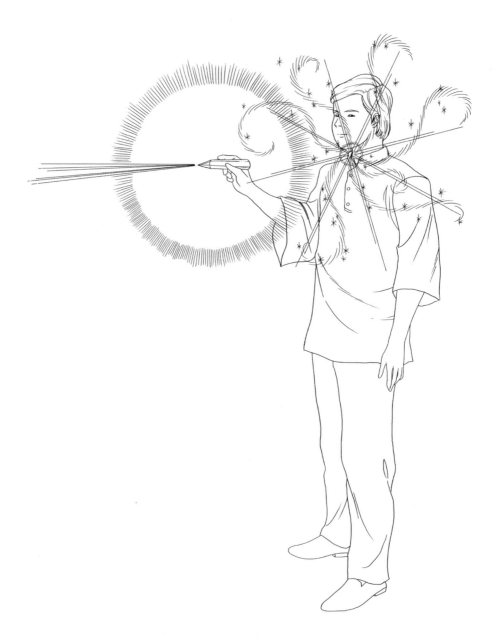

Fig. 5-2   Throat-hand chakras technique using a crystal

2. Blue prana — cooling, contracting, soothing, inhibiting, stabilizing

Procedure:

1. Put the chakral activator on your receiving hand, and the laser crystal on your projecting hand.

2. Connect your tongue to your palate.

3. Concentrate on your throat and the tips of the projecting fingers.

4. To project light whitish green prana or light whitish blue prana, use the same technique to produce light whitish red prana.

CROWN-HAND CHAKRAS TECHNIQUE

The crown-hand chakras technique uses the crown chakra as the source chakra and the hand chakra as the projecting chakra. (*See Fig. 5-3*)

This technique is done by concentrating on the crown chakra and the projecting hand chakra. Be aware of your crown or the top of your head, concentrating simultaneously on the tips of the projecting fingers. Imagine or visualize the required color prana(s).

By using the crown-hand chakras technique, you can project the following color pranas:

1. Ordinary violet prana — regenerating, activating; has properties of all color pranas

Fig. 5-3   Crown-hand chakras technique using a crystal

2. Electric violet — has intelligence of its own; more potent than ordinary violet prana

3. Subtle yellow prana — regenerating

4. Gold — has the same properties as electric violet

The crown chakra contains ordinary violet prana, electric violet, gold, subtle yellow prana and other color pranas. The subtle yellow prana from the crown chakra has a regenerating effect while the gross yellow prana from the basic chakra is used mainly for the healing of broken bones and torn tendons.

Procedure:

1. Put the chakral activator on your receiving hand, and the laser crystal on your projecting hand.

2. Connect your tongue to your palate.

3. Concentrate on your crown or the top of your head and the tips of the projecting fingers.

4. To produce ordinary light whitish violet prana, project luminous white light and add light violet on the periphery.

5. To produce electric violet, project brilliant white light and add light violet on the periphery.

6. To produce golden prana, visualize and project golden light.

How to use color pranas

*(The following text is taken from the book **Advanced Pranic Healing** by **Master Choa Kok Sui.**)*

Color prana is more specialized and more potent than white prana. Using color prana instead of white prana is just like approaching a specialist instead of a general practitioner. When using color pranas, avoid projecting dark color prana since it may have adverse effects. In some cases, it may have a reverse reaction. For example, light red prana has a strengthening effect but dark red prana has an overwhelming effect and will weaken the treated part. *When projecting a color prana, it is safer and more effective to use light or pastel color.*

The potency of a light color prana can be further diluted by combining it with white prana. For example, one can visualize the projected prana as luminous white at the core with light red at the periphery to strengthen an organ. *It is better and safer to combine a color prana of lighter shade with white prana. White prana is the harmonizing prana.* It is harmonizing in the sense that it provides the other color pranas required in healing and it redistributes excess color pranas from the treated area to other parts of the body. In general, better, faster, and safer results are obtained by combining white prana (about 70%) with light color prana (about 30%) than just light color prana since white prana provides the other color pranas required in healing. On rare occasions, if necessary, the author uses light color prana for more potent effects.

When energizing with color pranas, it is safer to flick the hand a few times before energizing with another color prana.

FOUR THINGS TO AVOID WHEN USING COLOR PRANAS

(The following information is drawn from the instructor's manual **Master Choa Kok Sui Advanced Pranic Healing Course***.)*

1. In general, do not use or project dark color pranas. It may produce adverse effects.

2. Orange prana should not be used on delicate parts or organs of the body or on the following conditions:

   a) Head and eyes — Projecting orange prana on the head and the eyes will damage the brain, and the eyes.

   b) Heart — Dark orange prana when applied to the heart will cause palpitations and other complications. Projecting light whitish orange on the heart should be done only by proficient pranic healers.

   c) Spleen chakra — This provides easy access to other chakras, including the chakras on the head. Therefore, do not energize the spleen with orange prana.

   d) Loose bowel movement or abdominal pain - In general, it is not advisable to use orange prana on patients with these conditions. Doing so will cause the condition to become worse.

   e)   Pregnant women.

   f)   Dying patients.

3. Do not project violet prana simultaneously with red prana, orange prana, or yellow prana. The effect is destructive.

4. Do not project electric violet prana simultaneously with any other color pranas. The effect is destructive.

How to Increase
the Power of Your Crystal

The power of a crystal can be increased by charging it with a tremendous amount of prana. A crystal that has been charged and one that has not been charged have the same activating effect on the chakras. The charged crystal, however, is still more powerful. In what sense is it more powerful? For example, by putting on the receiving hand an uncharged chakral activator, a person's basic chakra which is about 3½ inches might be activated to about 5 or 6 inches. A charged crystal will still have the same degree of activation but the density of pranic energy in the chakras, the energy body, and the aura is several times more compared to the uncharged crystal. The intensity of the pranic energy that it absorbs and projects is also several times more. By using a charged chakral activator, you can draw in and project much more pranic energy compared to an uncharged crystal. A 200-gram crystal that has been charged is much more powerful than a 400- or 500-gram crystal that has not been charged.

To maintain or to increase the potency of the charged crystal, it is necessary to cleanse it regularly, since it becomes contaminated with dirty energy, especially from the wearer. In normal daily activities and also during healing sessions, the wearer may sometimes experience wholesome emotions as well as a lot of stress, anger, irritation and other negative emotions. The crystal, being a subtle energy condenser, will absorb different types of energies, including dirty energy. Once contaminated, the potency of the charged crystal is reduced substantially.

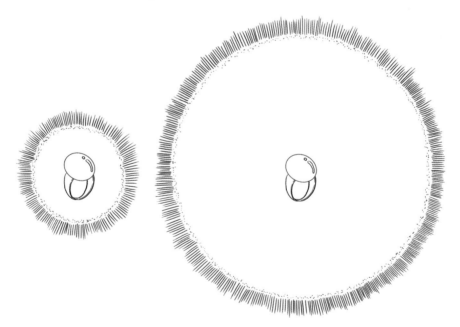

Fig. 6-1   A ring with a crystal before and after consecration

Fig. 6-2   Using consecrated rings with crystals to increase instantly one's healing power

What is the difference between charging and consecrating? In charging, the healer simply puts ordinary pranic energies into the crystal. Since a crystal is a subtle energy condenser, you can energize it by means of pranic breathing. A crystal also has consciousness; therefore, you can instruct the crystal to absorb pranic energy from the sun, the air and the earth or with the aid of nature spirits. Consecration, on the other hand, is not only charging the crystal with ordinary pranic energies but also with divine healing energy. This is done with help from higher beings and with the blessings of the Supreme Being.

Is the potency of a consecrated crystal different from a charged crystal? A consecrated crystal is more powerful than a charged crystal. The consecrated crystal not only increases the density or intensity of pranic energy in the chakras, the energy body, and the aura; it also increases the activating effect of the crystal on the chakras by 30-50 percent or more, depending on the spiritual development and skill of the person consecrating the crystal. (*See Fig. 6-1 & 6-2*)

A small crystal about a few grams only can be made into a powerful chakral activator just by consecrating it properly. It can be made even more powerful than a 150-gram quartz crystal that has not been charged with prana. Consecrated properly, a small crystal can be worn as a ring or pendant to increase instantly one's healing power. *A six-pointed star quartz crystal is highly recommended for use as a pendant to increase one's healing power. Ordinary crystals tend to activate the lower chakras more than the upper chakras. A six-pointed crystal activates both the lower and upper chakras evenly because of the nature of its geometric pattern.*

CHARGING A CRYSTAL THROUGH PRANIC BREATHING

One method of charging a crystal is by pranic breathing. This method is suitable for people who do not believe in the existence of nature spirits, angels, and higher beings.

1. Cleanse your crystal thoroughly using the salt solution technique and electric violet light.

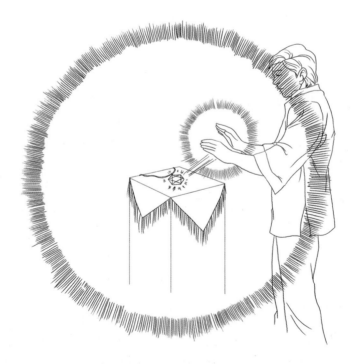

Fig. 6-3 A six-pointed star quartz crystal before and after charging through pranic breathing.

2. Do five cycles of pranic breathing.

3. Direct your palms towards the crystal. Continue doing pranic breathing for about 20 cycles and charge the crystal with pranic energy. *(See Fig. 6-3)*

4. Simultaneously instruct the crystal to absorb the pranic energy you are projecting.

5. Stabilize the projected pranic energy.

CHARGING A CRYSTAL WITH SOLAR, AIR AND EARTH PRANAS

You can further increase the potency of the charged crystal by instructing it to absorb pranic energy from the sun, the air and the earth. Look for a clean place where the crystal can be left for several hours without being disturbed or stolen. Preferably, there should be a few people or no people at all near the place because the crystal may compete with people in absorbing pranic energy.

Procedure:

1. After you have charged your crystal, you may increase its potency further by instructing it mentally or verbally to absorb pranic energy from the sun, the air and the earth, and to continue absorbing pranic energy until it is instructed to stop.

2. The crystal must be exposed to the sun and it should preferably touch the earth or the grass. Make sure there is

no septic tank below the ground. You do not want your crystal to be contaminated with very dirty energy.

3. You can program your crystal in the morning and go back to it much later. Once the crystal has been highly charged, instruct it to stop absorbing pranic energy.

4. Stabilize the charged crystal.

Note: *The charged crystal has to be cleansed and recharged regularly in order to maintain or increase its potency. Depending on the frequency of use, cleansing and recharging once a month or once every three months may be sufficient.*

CONSECRATION: CHARGING AND PROGRAMMING CRYSTALS IN AN OPEN AREA

Consecration is more powerful than using pranic breathing and/ or instructing crystals to charge themselves with pranic energy. Consecrating crystals is best done in a clean open area since they will also be absorbing pranic energy from the sun, the air and the earth.

It is a prerequisite that the practitioner believes in God or The Universal Supreme Being, the higher beings, the holy angels, the beings of light and the nature spirits.

Before consecrating your crystals they must be cleansed thoroughly. In the old Christian rituals, cleansing was called exorcism. This is why if you study some of the Christian

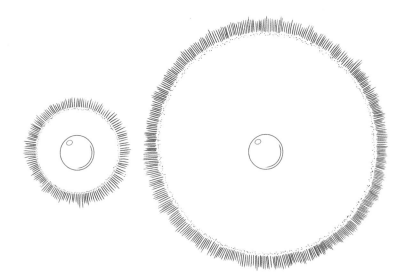

Fig. 6-4   A chakral activator before and after consecration

manuscripts or books on rituals, they discussed exorcism of the materials that were used in theurgy. Exorcism in its strictest sense simply means cleansing a substance of dirty energy, negative beings, negative thought entities, negative psychic impressions, previous psychic impressions and previous programs. "Cleansing" is a modern term for the much misunderstood and outdated "exorcism". (*See Fig. 6-4 & 6-5*)

Part 1 - Invoking the Help of the Supreme Being

Put the crystals on the ground and request divine blessings from God or the Supreme Being:

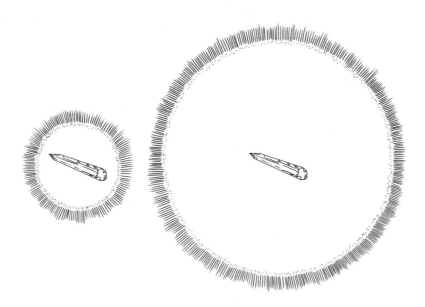

Fig. 6-5   A laser crystal before and after consecration

> *To the Supreme Being, thank You for charging these crystals with Your divine blessings, divine love and mercy, divine healing energy, and divine healing power. With thanks and in full faith.*

Tell the crystals:

> *Absorb the blessings and the pranic energy now.*

Wait for a few minutes then continue with part 2.

Part 2 - Invoking the Help of the Higher Beings

Part II of charging your crystals is done by invoking the help of healing angels, healing ministers and other holy beings:

To the holy masters, holy gurus, healing angels, healing ministers, beings of light, and all the great ones, thank you for charging these crystals with divine blessings, divine love, divine mercy and divine healing energy. With thanks and in full faith.

Instruct the crystals:

Absorb the blessings and the pranic energy now.

Wait for a few minutes before going to part 3.

Part 3 - Charging with Sun, Air and Earth Pranas

Part 3 is charging the crystals with pranic energy from the sun, the air and the earth:

To the nature spirits and angles of the sun, the air, and the earth, thank you for charging these crystals with sun prana, air prana and earth prana. With thanks and in full faith.

Instruct the crystals:

Absorb and store pranic energy from the sun, the air and the earth right now. Absorb only clean, healthy pranic energy. Continue absorbing until you are instructed to stop.

Wait for a few minutes before proceeding to part 4.

Part 4 - Automatic Recharging

To recharge the crystals automatically, instruct them to draw in pranic energy from the healing angels, healing ministers, beings of light, and the great ones when they are being used for healing. With a laser crystal, instruct it to recharge automatically when it is projecting energy.

Giving the crystals the proper instructions is very important. Do not tell the crystals to absorb pranic energy from the surroundings only. If you give such an instruction, they may absorb or draw out pranic energy even from people within the surroundings. This may cause serious health problems to those living within the area, including pets and plants. When instructing the crystals, do not also specify the name of any guru. Unless the Guru grants permission, using the Guru's name is unethical.

Mentally say to your crystals:

> *You will automatically draw in pranic energy from the assigned healing angels, healing ministers, beings of light, and the great ones everytime you are used for healing. So be it. So be it. So be it.*

It is important to keep your crystal clean. If it is clean, it can continue to absorb pranic energy and will thereby be recharged automatically.

Part 5 - Expressing Gratitude

After consecrating the crystals, it is important to give thanks.

To the Supreme Being or God,

> *Thank You again for the Blessings.*
> *With thanks and in full faith.*

To the healing angels, healing ministers, beings of light, and the great ones,

> *Thank you again for the divine blessings.*
> *With thanks and in full faith.*

To the angels and nature spirits of the sun, the air and the earth,

> *Thank you again for the divine blessings.*
> *With thanks and in full faith.*

Part 6 - End of Consecration of Crystals

1. Mentally or verbally instruct the crystals, *"Stop absorbing more energy now. So be it."*

2. Stabilize the absorbed energy by "painting" it with light blue.

3. When not in use, wrap the consecrated crystals in a silk cloth.

HOW TO USE THE CONSECRATED CRYSTAL

1. Say a short prayer, using your own words to ask for divine blessings and divine healing or you may use the prayer given in Chapter 4.

2. If the patient is religious or spiritual, you may also request him or her to say a short prayer. This will make the healing more effective.

3. Connect your tongue to your palate.

4. You may use the chakral activator on the receiving hand and the consecrated laser crystal on the projecting hand. Or you may use the consecrated laser crystal only. Hold the consecrated laser crystal between your thumb, forefinger, and middle finger with the receiving end outside your palm so that it can get pranic energy easily from the healing angels, healing ministers, beings of light, and the great ones.

   You can also use the consecrated crystal to project color pranas. When using a highly charged or properly consecrated crystal, do not use too much will while you are healing. Be gentle and do not overenergize your patients.

5. Stabilize and cut the etheric link between you and the patient.

6. Say a short prayer of thanksgiving.

7. Instruct the patient to also say a short prayer of thanksgiving.

8. Cleanse the crystal with water and salt.

More About Pranic Crystal Healing

In the study of esoteric sciences, exercising discrimination is necessary. Do not accept everything blindly because this can result in confusion.

CRYSTAL PENDULUM

There are definitely many good books written about crystal healing; they are informative and practical. But some crystal healing books contain many doubtful teachings. Let us take for instance a crystal pendulum. Some healers use the crystal pendulum for diagnosis and healing. They believe that if there is something wrong with a chakra, the crystal pendulum will move counterclockwise and will continue to do so until the chakra normalizes. If the crystal moves clockwise, the chakra is supposed to be functioning properly. This may or may not be true.

A person with pranic healing background will realize that when a crystal pendulum turns counterclockwise, it is cleansing or extracting the diseased energy from the affected chakra. When seen clairvoyantly, the chakra is turning predominantly counterclockwise, and in the process expelling the dirty energy to the crystal pendulum. If the crystal is turned clockwise, the chakra will also turn predominantly clockwise, thereby absorbing pranic energy from the surroundings, the dirty crystal and the healer.

The clockwise motion of the crystal pendulum has an energizing effect while the counterclockwise motion has an expelling effect. The idea that the clockwise motion of the crystal pendulum is an indication that the chakra is normal, and the counterclockwise motion is not normal may be doubtful.

But you can definitely use a crystal pendulum to heal a patient. Ask the patient to lie down, then swing the pendulum counterclockwise and will the crystal to absorb, extract, disintegrate and expel the dirty energy. What do you do when you want to energize? Use a clean, charged pendulum and move it clockwise to energize the chakra. But why use a pendulum when it is easier to use a charged laser crystal?

JEWELRY: PSYCHIC IMPREGNATION

In many countries, it is a common practice for parents or grandparents to hand down Jewelry or pieces of Jewelry to their children. This is good but you must understand that Jewelry which used to belong to another person has been impregnated with certain qualities or energies that might not be wholesome. Therefore, it is necessary to cleanse the Jewelry with the use of water or alcohol and electric violet light.

A patient who used to wear a ring that her mother had given her had a physical and psychological disorder. The mother had worn the ring when she was suffering and dying from cancer. The ring was, of course, impregnated with much pain, psychological discomfort, depression and pessimism. As a result, the daughter became psychologically imbalanced and physically sick. When the ring was removed from her finger, she immediately felt partial relief.

In buying Jewelry, you must be aware that the Jewelry has been handled by so many people and in the process impregnated with unwholesome thoughts and dirty energy. Therefore, it has to be cleansed with water or alcohol, and electric violet light. Using salt solution is not advisable because it may physically damage the precious stone.

Fig. 7-1 Laying on of consecrated crystals

LAYING ON OF CONSECRATED CRYSTALS

Instead of having to do too much work, a healer can simply tell the patient to lie down, and put several consecrated crystals over the affected parts and chakras or all over the body. Instruct the crystals to clean and energize the affected chakras and organs, and also to energize the whole body. (*See Fig. 7-1*)

Do not use a consecrated crystal on the front heart area. This can cause the heart to become congested with too much pranic energy which can lead to palpitation or chest pain. Place it at the back of the heart.

You can use crystals in the form of pebbles. They are relatively inexpensive. Clear quartz crystal, rose quartz crystal and other color crystals can be used for laying on patients. Clear quartz crystal, rose quartz crystal and green crystal are relatively safer and easier to use. If you want to use crystals with other colors, it is better to have a background in advanced pranic healing.

When you are laying consecrated crystals on a patient, it is advisable to get feedback regularly; ask him or her to describe his or her feelings and also any unusual sensation or experience. Practice caution.

PROCEDURE FOR LAYING ON OF CONSECRATED CRYSTALS

Practicing laying on of consecrated crystals should not be done on pregnant women. Children have small chakras; in general, laying them with consecrated crystals may not be advisable.

1. Let the patient lie down and ask him or her to relax.

2. Instruct the patient to connect the tongue to the palate.

3. Light sandalwood incense. This is to further disintegrate the diseased energy that will be expelled from the patient. Make sure that the room is relatively big and well ventilated.

4. Ask for divine blessings. You may use the prayer in Chapter 4.

5. Put a clear quartz crystal, or green crystal at the back of the heart. Instruct the crystal to extract, absorb, disintegrate and expel the dirty energy from the front and back heart chakras, the physical heart, and the lungs. Instruct the crystal to energize simultaneously the front and back heart chakras, the physical heart, the lungs and the whole body and to continue doing so until it is instructed to stop.

    It is advisable to use a green crystal on the back heart because it has a cleansing and decongesting effect. For instance, if a person's heart has a partial obstruction, the diseased energy that clogs the arteries of the heart can be gradually disintegrated with the use of a green crystal.

6. Put a clear quartz crystal, or rose quartz crystal, or green crystal on the solar plexus chakra. Instruct the crystal to extract, absorb, disintegrate and expel the dirty and diseased energies from the solar plexus chakra. Instruct the crystal to energize simultaneously the solar plexus chakra and the whole body.

7. Put a clear quartz crystal, or an amethyst crystal, or green crystal on the crown chakra. Instruct the crystal to extract, absorb, disintegrate and expel dirty and diseased energies from the crown, the brain, the pineal gland, and to energize simultaneously the crown, the brain, the pineal gland and the whole body.

8. Put a clear quartz crystal, or amethyst crystal, or green crystal on the forehead chakra. Instruct the crystal to extract, absorb, disintegrate and expel dirty and diseased energies from the forehead chakra, the pineal gland and the nervous system. Instruct the crystal to energize simultaneously the forehead chakra, the pineal gland, the nervous system and the whole body.

9. Put a clear quartz crystal, or amethyst crystal, or green crystal on the ajna chakra. Instruct the crystal to extract, absorb, disintegrate and expel dirty and diseased energies from the ajna chakra, the nose, and the pituitary gland, and to energize simultaneously the ajna chakra, the pituitary gland,

the endocrine glands and the whole body.

10. Put a clear quartz crystal, or rose quartz crystal, or green crystal on the throat chakra. Instruct the crystal to extract, absorb, disintegrate and expel dirty and diseased energies from the throat chakra, the thyroid gland, the trachea and the esophagus and to energize simultaneously the throat chakra, the thyroid gland, the trachea, the esophagus and the whole body.

11. Put a clear quartz crystal on the navel chakra. Instruct the crystal to extract, absorb, disintegrate and expel dirty and diseased energies from the navel chakra, the small intestine and the large intestine. Instruct the crystal to energize simultaneously the navel chakra, the small intestine, the large intestine and the whole body.

12. If the spleen chakra is very dirty, you may also put a consecrated clear quartz crystal on the back spleen chakra. Instruct the crystal to extract, absorb, disintegrate and expel dirty and diseased energies from the spleen chakra and the physical spleen, and to energize simultaneously the spleen chakra gently and the whole body. Be cautious.

13. Put a clear quartz crystal, or green crystal on the sex chakra. Instruct the crystal to extract, absorb, disintegrate and expel dirty and diseased energies from the sex chakra, sex organs and urinary bladder and to energize simultaneously the sex

chakra, sex organs, urinary bladder and the whole body.

14. Put a clear quartz crystal between the legs near the basic chakra. Instruct the crystal to extract, absorb, disintegrate and expel dirty and diseased energies from the basic chakra and the whole body. Instruct it to energize simultaneously the basic chakra and the whole body.

15. Put a clear quartz crystal on each armpit. Instruct the crystal to extract, absorb, disintegrate and expel dirty and diseased energies from each armpit and the whole body, and to energize simultaneously each armpit and the whole body.

16. Put a clear quartz crystal under each elbow. Instruct the crystal to extract, absorb, disintegrate and expel dirty and diseased energies from each elbow and the whole body, and to energize simultaneously each elbow and the whole body.

17. Put a clear quartz crystal on each hand. Instruct the crystal to extract, absorb, disintegrate and expel dirty and diseased energies from each hand and the whole body, and to energize them simultaneously and the whole body.

18. Put a clear quartz crystal on the side of each hip. Instruct the crystal to extract, absorb, disintegrate and expel dirty and diseased energies from the hips, and to energize them simultaneously and the whole body.

19. Put a clear quartz crystal under the back of each knee. Instruct the crystal to extract, absorb, disintegrate and expel dirty and diseased energies from the back of each knee and the whole body, and to energize them simultaneously and the whole body.

20. Put a clear quartz crystal on the soles of the feet. Instruct the crystal to extract, absorb, disintegrate and expel dirty and diseased energies from each sole and the whole body, and to energize them simultaneously and the whole body.

Let the patient lie down for about 20 minutes or longer. In most cases, the patient will have quite a powerful or dramatic experience. If the patient is having an unpleasant experience, remove the crystals immediately. Instruct them to stop cleansing and energizing now and put them in the salt solution.

At the end of the procedure, remove all the crystals and tell them to stop cleansing and energizing. Put them in the salt solution. Instruct them to expel completely all the absorbed dirty and diseased energies into the salt solution.

PROPERTIES OF COLOR CRYSTALS

Let us talk about color crystals. The color of a crystal affects to a substantial degree the color prana that comes out of it. The energy projected by a red crystal is light red. With amethyst, it is violet prana. Rose quartz gives off pink prana while clear quartz emits white prana. But you can also project other colors from a clear crystal, depending on the particular color you need. Unless you want a specific color like green, then use green crystal.

The properties of color crystals correspond to the properties of the different color pranas. To be able to use color crystals properly,

Color	Physical Properties	Psychological Properties
Red	Warm and strengthening	Bravery, courage, dynamic activity, aggressiveness and others
Orange	Expelling (Sweating, urinating, bowel movement, cleansing)	Enthusiasm, fanaticism, and others
Yellow	Cementing	Higher mental activity
Green	Breaking down and digesting	Tactfulness, diplomacy
Blue	Cooling and inhibiting	Lower mental activity or concrete thinking
Violet	Has properties of all the above	Spirituality
Pink	Attractive, soothing and harmonizing	Love

it is necessary to have a good background in Advanced Pranic Healing.

The following are the physical and psychological properties of color crystals :

Rings or pendants with color crystals can be used to affect the mood of a person. If you have a patient who is depressed or timid, request the patient to wear a red or peach crystal as a ring or pendant. If you want a person to be calm, advise him or her to wear a rose quartz pendant or a blue crystal. However, the stone or the crystal has to be cleansed thoroughly before it is used. The crystal to be worn can be charged and psychically impregnated to increase its potency.

As a reminder to the reader, it is important that the precious and semi-precious stones or crystals must preferably not be sharp or pointed at the bottom. This will cause pranic energy to leak out from the energy body. The bottom must be rounded or flat.

Besides healing, crystals have many practical and esoteric uses. The author may seriously consider writing another book on crystals.

I hope you have enjoyed reading the book and have benefited from it. My best wishes to all readers. May God bless each one of you with peace, happiness, clarity of mind, good health, prosperity, and spirituality.

Sensitizing the Hands

(The following text is taken from the book *The Ancient Science and Art of Pranic Healing* by **Master Choa Kok Sui.**)

Since it takes considerable time to develop the auric sight, you should at least try to sensitize your hands in order to feel the bioplasmic energy field or the inner aura. This will enable you to determine which areas of the patient's bioplasmic body are depleted or congested. (*See Fig. 8-1*)

Procedure:

1. Place your hands about three inches apart facing each other. Do not tense, just relax.

2. Concentrate on feeling the centers of your palms. Be aware of the centers of your palms and the surrounding area for about 5-10 minutes; inhale and exhale slowly and rhythmically. Concentration is facilitated by pressing the centers of the palms with your thumbs before starting. By concentrating on the centers of the palms, the hand chakras are activated, thereby sensitizing the hands or enabling the hands to feel subtle energy or matter.

    Eighty to ninety percent of you will be able to feel a tingling sensation, heat, pressure or rhythmic pulsation between the palms on the first try. It is important to feel the pressure or rhythmic pulsation.

3. Proceed immediately to scanning after sensitizing your hands.

4. Practice sensitizing your hands for about a month. In general, your hands should be more or less permanently sensitized after a month of practice.

5. Do not be discouraged if you do not feel anything on the first try. Continue your practice; it is likely that you will be able to feel these subtle sensations on the fourth session. Keeping an open mind and concentrating properly is very important.

Fig. 8-1   Sensitizing the hands

Scanning the Inner Aura

(The following text is taken also from the *The Ancient Science and Art of Pranic Healing* by *Master Choa Kok Sui*.)

PROCEDURE FOR SCANNING THE INNER AURA

1. To feel the inner aura with one or both hands, put your hand(s) about 12 inches away from the patient's body. Walk gradually towards the patient while simultaneously moving your hand(s) back and forth. The inner aura is usually about fives inches thick. Concentrate on the centers of your palms when scanning in order that the hand chakras may remain or be further activated, thereby making the hands sensitive to subtle energy or matter. (*See Fig. 8-2*)

2. Scan the subject from head to foot and from front to back. Scan the left part and right part of the body. For example, scan the left and right ears or scan the right and left lungs. The inner auras of the right and left parts of the body should have about the same thickness when scanned. If one part is bigger or smaller than the other part, then there is something wrong with it. When, for

Fig. 8-2   Scanning the inner aura with the hands

instance, the ears of a patient were scanned and the inner aura of the left ear was found to be about five inches thick while that of the right ear was only about two inches thick, it turned out, after questioning the patient, that the right ear had been partially deaf for the past 17 years.

3. Special attention should be given to the major chakras, the vital organs, and the spine. In many cases, a portion of the spine is usually either congested or depleted even if the patient does not complain of back problems.

4. In scanning the throat area, the chin should be raised upward in order to get accurate scanning. The inner aura of the chin tends to interfere or camouflage the actual condition of the throat.

5. Scanning of the lungs should be done at the back and the sides rather than the front in order to get accurate results. The nipples have two mini chakras that tend to interfere in the proper scanning of the lungs. A more advanced technique is to scan the lungs at the front, the back and the sides with two fingers instead of the entire hand.

6. Special attention should be given to the solar plexus chakra since many diseases of emotional origin negatively affect it.

INTERPRETING RESULTS FROM
SCANNING THE INNER AURA

1. In scanning your patient, you will notice that there are
    hollows or protrusions in some areas of the patient's inner
    aura. A hollow area is caused by *pranic depletion*. The affected
    part is depleted of prana or has insufficient prana. The
    surrounding fine meridians are partially or severely blocked,
    preventing fresh

    prana from other parts to flow freely and vitalize the
    affected part. In pranic depletion, the affected chakra is
    depleted and filled with dirty diseased bioplasmic matter.
    Usually, it is partially underactivated.

2. When an area protrudes, it means there is *pranic congestion
    or bioplasmic congestion*. Too much prana and bioplasmic
    matter on the affected area causes the surrounding fine
    meridians to be partially or severely blocked. The excess
    prana and bioplasmic matter cannot flow out freely. This
    congested prana and bioplasmic matter become devitalized
    and diseased after a certain period of time because fresh
    prana cannot flow in freely or its inflow is greatly reduced,
    and the devitalized matter cannot flow out freely or its
    outflow is greatly reduced. In pranic congestion, the affected
    chakra is congested and filled with diseased bioplasmic
    matter. Usually, it is partially overactivated.

3. An affected part may have pranic congestion and pranic depletion simultaneously. It means that a portion of the affected part is hollow and another portion is protruding. For instance, a liver is congested or protruding on the left portion and is hollow or depleted on the right portion. Another example is that a portion of the left heart is congested or protruding while a portion of the right heart is severely depleted.

4. The smaller the inner aura, the more severe is the pranic depletion. The bigger the protrusion of the inner aura, the more congested is the affected part. The smaller or bigger is the inner aura of the diseased part, the more severe is the ailment.

5. An area may have a *temporary pranic surplus* in which case there is nothing wrong with it. For instance, a person who has been sitting for a long time when scanned may have a big protrusion of the inner aura around the buttocks area. Since the surrounding meridians are not blocked, the condition normalizes after a short period of time.

6. An area may have *temporary pranic reduction* in which case there is also nothing wrong with it. An altercation that has just occurred is likely to cause a temporary pranic reduction around the solar plexus area. After a few hours of rest, the condition will normalize. But habitual altercation or anger

Fig. 8-3   Scanning the inner aura with the fingers

may cause pranic depletion around the solar plexus area, resulting in abdominal ailment and possibly heart disease.

7. The physical condition of the patient should be carefully observed and the patient should be questioned or interviewed thoroughly before making any conclusion.

8. Diseases manifest first on the bioplasmic body before manifesting on the visible physical body. There are cases in which there is pranic depletion or pranic congestion in the inner aura of an affected part although medical findings would show negative result or normalcy of the part. In this case, the disease has not yet manifested on the visible physical body. *Therefore, pranic healing should be applied on the ailment before it can manifest physically.*

SCANNING WITH THE FINGERS

After sensitizing your hands, scan your own palm with your two fingers. Move your fingers slowly and slightly back and forth to feel the inner aura of your palm. Try to feel the thickness of your palm and the different layers of the inner aura. Practice also scanning of your palm with one finger. Always concentrate on the tips of your fingers when scanning with them. This will activate or further activate the mini finger chakras, thereby sensitizing the fingers. (*See Fig. 8-3*)

When scanning with your palms and fingers, always concentrate on the centers of your palms and on the tips of your fingers. This will cause the hand chakras and the finger chakras to remain activated or become more activated, increasing the sensitivity of your palms and fingers.

Being able to scan with the palms is not sufficient. You must also learn to scan with your fingers. This is required in locating or proper scanning of small troubled spots which is difficult to do with the palm. The palm may only feel the healthier surrounding areas around the small troubled spot. Small troubled spots are "camouflaged" by the healthier parts.

For instance, a person with eye problems usually have pranic depletion in the eyes while the inner auras of the surrounding area may be normal. Since the palm is quite big and the inner aura of the eyes is about two inches in diameter, it is likely that the palms may feel only the healthy areas of the eyebrows and forehead without becoming aware of the small troubled spots. This could be avoided if the fingers were used in scanning. The spinal column should also be scanned by using one or two fingers in order to locate small troubled spots.

Miraculous Divine Healing
Technique

In miraculous healing, the patient has high reverence for and is very receptive to God and the higher beings. This state of reverence and receptiveness causes the energy body to produce a lot of ordinary violet prana. This is why the color violet is connected with spirituality. Ordinary violet prana makes the energy body and physical body extremely responsive to divine healing energy or electric violet light. This is how miraculous healing occurs. Ordinary people who are skeptical and have no respect for God and the higher beings are not able to produce sufficient amount of ordinary violet prana. When electric violet light is projected, the response of the energy body and the physical body is minimal, sometimes none at all. As a result, the rate of healing is slow or there is no healing at all. By energizing the patient with ordinary violet prana, then electric violet prana, we are able to duplicate the conditions that are similar or needed to produce miraculous divine healing.

This technique is very powerful. Preferably, it should not be applied on the following chakras:

1. Meng mein chakra — Applying it on the meng mein chakra may cause hypertension.

2. Preferably not on the basic chakra, sex chakra and the perineum minor chakra — It may overactivate the basic chakra and make the person restless. It has also the tendency of awakening not in the proper manner the kundalini energy. This energy is located somewhere near the base of the spine. Improper awakening of the kundalini energy may cause physical and psychological problems. When used on the sex chakra, it may become highly overactivated and thus may increase the sex drive tremendously. This may cause serious marital problems.

3. The spleen chakra — It may cause the energy body to become congested.

4. Do not also apply it on the front heart chakra or the chest area because it may cause the heart chakra to become highly overactivated and congested, and may result in physical heart problems.

The ratio of ordinary light whitish violet prana to light electric violet prana is four is to one (4:1). As the patient becomes stronger, the ratio can be increased to three is to one (3:1). The proper application of this technique has to be learned through actual experience. Overenergizing the patient may cause radical reaction and thus make the condition worse. If the patient is insufficiently energized, he may not get well or the healing may not be as miraculous as expected. The healer must be sensitive to inner guidance in order to use this technique properly. It is advisable to invoke for divine blessings before using this technique.

This technique is to be used by experienced advanced pranic healers, not by beginners.

Master Choa Kok Sui Audio and Video CDs

Meditation on Twin Hearts
for Peace and Illumination

Meditation on Twin Hearts
with Self-Pranic Healing

Meditation on Twin Hearts
for Psychological Health and Well-Being

Meditation on the Soul

Meditation on Loving-Kindness

Wesak Festival Meditation

Amen

Om: The Sound of Stillness

Om Shanti

Om Mani Padme Hum
The Mantra of Compassion and Mercy

Meditation on the Lord's Prayer:
Universal and Kabbalistic Versions

Inner Purification
The Blue Triangle Technique

Om Namo Rama Om

Gayatri Mantra

Lakshmi Gayatri Mantra

Om Namah Shivaya Om

Arhatic Yoga Kundalini Meditation:
Meditation on the Inner Breath
(for Arhatic Yogis only)

Arhatic Dhyan
(for Arhatic Yogis only)

Arhatic Sadhana
for Arhatic Yoga Meditation Centers

The Existence of God is Self-Evident
(Audio Book)

Meditation on Twin Hearts
(Video)

Master Choa Kok Sui Courses

1. Basic Pranic Healing
2. Advanced Pranic Healing
3. Pranic Psychotherapy
4. Pranic Crystal Healing
5. Pranic Self-Healing
6. Practical Psychic Self-Defense
7. Kriyashakti for Prosperity and Success
8. Pranic Feng Shui
9. The Spiritual Essence of Man
10. Achieving Oneness with the Higher Soul
11. Universal & Kabbalistic Meditation on the Lord's Prayer
12. Arhatic Yoga
13. Arhatic Sexual Alchemy
14. Clairvoyance
15. Spiritual Business Management
16. Inner Teachings of Hinduism Revealed
17. Inner Teachings of Christianity Revealed
18. Om Mani Padme Hum
19. Inner Teachings of Buddhism Revealed
20. Superbrain Yoga
21. Pranic Facial Rejuvenation

The course titles above are registered *Service Marks.*
The course contents are all copyrighted.

For more information contact:
INSTITUTE FOR INNER STUDIES, INC.
Postal Address: Suite 808 G/F Island Plaza Salcedo Bldg.
105 Leviste St., Salcedo Village
1227 Makati City, Philippines
Tel. Nos. (63-2) 819-18-74; 810-2808
Fax No. (63-2) 731-38-28
E-mail: info@globalpranichealing.com
Website: www.globalpranichealing.com

For books, audio and video compact discs, and MCKS aura
and chakra cleansing spray please order at: **order@globalpranichealing.com**
For certificates and licenses, please order at: **iis_lc@globalpranichealing.com**

Pranic Healing
Centers and Organizations

Institute for Inner Studies, Inc.
Postal Address: Suite 808 G/F Island Plaza
Salcedo Bldg., 105 Leviste St., Salcedo Village
1227 Makati City, Philippines
Tel. Nos. (63-2) 819-1874; 810-2808
Fax No. (63-2) 731-3828
E-mail: info@globalpranichealing.com
Website: www.globalpranichealing.com

World Pranic Healing Foundation
Unit 2210 Medical Plaza Ortigas Condominium
San Miguel Avenue, Ortigas Center, Pasig City 1605
Metro Manila Philippines
Postal Address: Suite 808 G/F Island Plaza
Salcedo Bldg., 105 Leviste St., Salcedo Village
1227 Makati City, Philippines
Tel. Nos. (63-2) 635-9732 to 34
Fax No. (63-2) 687-4726
E-mail: worldpranichealingmanila@gmail.com
Website: www.worldpranichealing.com

MCKS Charitable Foundation, Inc.
Unit 2210 Medical Plaza Ortigas
San Miguel Avenue, Ortigas Center, Pasig City 1605
Metro Manila Philippines
Tel. Nos.: (632) 635-9732 up to 34
Fax No.: (632) 687-4726
E-mail: mckscharitable@gmail.com
Website: www.mckscharitable.org

Pranic Healing International Addresses

Pranic Healing services, courses, audio and video compact discs are available in Pranic Healing centers and organizations in the countries listed below.

For specific contact details, and complete, updated country list, please visit: **www.globalpranichealing.com**

ARGENTINA	GREECE	PERU
ARUBA	GUATEMALA	PHILIPPINES
AUSTRALIA	GUYANA	POLAND
AUSTRIA	HONDURAS	PORTUGAL
BELGIUM	HONG KONG	PUERTO RICO
BELIZE	HUNGARY	ROMANIA
BENIN	INDIA	RUSSIA
BOLIVIA	INDONESIA	SCOTLAND
BOSNIA-HERZEGOVINA	IRAN	SINGAPORE
BRAZIL	IRELAND	SLOVAKIA
BHUTAN	ISRAEL	SLOVENIA
BULGARIA	ITALY	SOUTH AFRICA
CANADA	JAPAN	SOUTH PACIFIC ISLAND
CARIBBEAN Region	JORDAN	SPAIN
CHILE	KAZAKHSTAN	SRI LANKA
COLOMBIA	KENYA	SWEDEN
COSTA RICA	KOREA	SWITZERLAND
CROATIA	LEBANON	SYRIA
CUBA	LITHUANIA	THAILAND
CYPRUS	MACEDONIA	TOGO
CZECH REPUBLIC	MALAYSIA	TURKEY
DENMARK	MAURITIUS	UKRAINE
DOMINICAN REPUBLIC	MEXICO	UNITED ARAB EMIRATES
ECUADOR	The NETHERLANDS	UNITED KINGDOM
EL SALVADOR	NEW ZEALAND	UNITED STATES of AMERICA
FIJI	NICARAGUA	URUGUAY
FINLAND	NIGERIA	VENEZUELA
FRANCE	OMAN	WEST AFRICA
GERMANY	PANAMA	
GHANA	PARAGUAY	

Index

Illustrations